WITCHCRAFT

A SECRET HISTORY

WITCHCRAFT

A SECRET HISTORY

MICHAEL STREETER

CONT

ENTS

INTRODUCTION

Witchcraft has been controversial throughout history. The very mention of the word excites strong emotions. For some people it conjures up the rather folksy image of the storybook elderly witch with her pointy hat, broomstick, black cat, and crooked smile. For others, all witches are evil, devil-worshipping enemies of society, whose very existence is a danger to our young people.

The popularity of witchcraft has never been greater, especially among young people, who are taking up the challenges of the craft in ever increasing numbers. Yet the current image of witchcraft, despite its popularity and all the cozy images of the commercialized Halloween, is still not particularly positive.

That, of course, should surprise no one. Throughout history witches have been badly represented by different societies; sometimes harmlessly, but more often with fatal results.

Witchcraft: A Secret History looks behind the scenes of this history—from Babylonian gods to King Solomon, from the Roman Empire to Puritan New England—to explain how and why witches got the reputation they have. Along the way it will chart how they have had to fight for their survival and for their identity. And it will reveal the story of how one elderly man sparked a revival that has made Witchcraft what it is today—one of the fastest-growing religions in North America and the rest of the Western world.

What Is Witchcraft?

But just what do we mean by "witchcraft" or "witch?" This is not an easy question to answer for the simple reason that in the course of history different layers of meanings have been attached to the words. Indeed, the word "witch" has been loaded with so many negative meanings for so long it is often impossible for people to react to it in any other way than badly. For many, the words "evil" and "witch" go together like ham and eggs.

Folk Magic

Let us begin by looking at some of the alternative meanings of witchcraft. One is that it is simple sorcery—in other words, the use of magic in casting spells, healing, telling the future, or influencing the weather. These spells may be used for good purposes or for bad, depending on the person who casts them.

This kind of sorcery, folk magic, or witchcraft has existed in just about all known societies at all times, though this book is concerned with the traditions that have helped shape witchcraft in Western culture. In English-speaking societies such people have been known as "cunning folk" or "wise women/men." They have existed since time immemorial, and such people still exist today. For them witchcraft is simply a craft, a use of magic for specific ends. Magic can be defined as using one's will to change consciousness and reality. Simple sorcery has no connections with religion.

∧ Éliphas Lévi's 1855 illustration of Baphomet, a Pagan deity revived in the nineteenth century as a figure of occultism and Satanism.

Diabolical Witchcraft

Another definition of witchcraft is the one that developed in the late Middle Ages and Renaissance, and which dominated Western culture for perhaps 250 years: witchcraft as the worship of the Devil. This definition arose out of Christian thinking and was part of the late medieval Church's obsessions with heresy. The reasoning was quite simple.

The world was divided between Good and Evil, God and the Devil— though God, of course, had the upper hand. The Devil had helpers in the form of spirits called demons, so anyone who invoked spirits other than in the Christian context was naturally in league with demons and thus the Devil. As people who performed magic (i.e. witches) often invoked spirits, this meant that witches were the Devil's allies. As this idea developed, much of the late medieval world considered that witches entered a formal pact with the Devil, had sex with him or his demons, and tried to oppose God's will. Therefore, they were the worst kind of heretics and had to be burned. This accounts for the large number of witch trials and executions in North America and particularly Europe from around 1450 to 1700. A few of those burned may have been simple sorcerers, as in our first definition; most had no connection with magic at all. None actually worshipped the Devil.

The idea of diabolical witches was an invention of its time, but one that has survived among many conservative Christians—thanks in part to misleading translations of the Bible.

Modern Witchcraft

The third definition is that used by many modern witches. In this, Witchcraft is a religion with a capital "W"; it is a mystery religion, which believes in one ultimate deity, but puts special emphasis on the female aspect of that deity in the form of the Goddess, and it reveres gods from the old pagan religions. At the same time, Witchcraft uses magic—which witches believe is part of the natural world around them and not something remote or "supernatural"—as part of their spiritual development and identity as witches.

Incidentally, modern witches reject the suggestion of Satanic associations on the understandable grounds that Satan/the Devil is a Christian concept; and witches worship neither the Christian God nor its Devil. Yet, to avoid the negative value still attached to Witchcraft, many practitioners refer to it as Wicca and to themselves as Wiccans—both words are revivals of the Old English term for witch.

This, then, is the definition of witchcraft broadly adopted by *A Secret History*, though the word is also used in historical context to mean what people said it meant at that time.

It should also be pointed out that, just as there is no evidence that witches worshipped the Devil in the late Middle Ages, there is equally no evidence that witches worshipped the old pagan gods then, either.

The modern religion of Wicca can thus be seen as a fusion of folk magic or sorcery with pagan worship, plus borrowings from ceremonial magic dating back to Egypt and Ancient Judaea.

This book ends with a close look at how this dramatic revival of Witchcraft occurred and how witches have been able to emerge slowly from the shadows where they have been forced to hide. Witchcraft now appears to have a bright future. To understand how it has got there, we first need to consider its secret, and often dark, history.

T H E

ANCIENT

WORLD

THE DAWN OF WITCHCRAFT

Most societies in the world have a tradition of witchcraft. Many societies also revered goddesses such as Ishtar and Isis, who were linked with magic and witchcraft. Meanwhile, the Hebrews developed the idea of an evil god or devil, which in turn came to be identified in Western culture with anyone who performed witchcraft.

Magic, Witchcraft, and Religion

The use of magic—in which the force of a person's will harnesses natural forces to influence events or outcomes—is common to most cultures in the world. At its most basic, such magic is not part of a religion, but could be referred to as simple magic in which certain acts are carried out to produce defined effects. This might be sticking a pin in the image of someone to cause harm to that person; or having sex in a newly sown wheat field to ensure that the coming harvest is a good one.

This form of folk magic is similar to that practiced by those so-called "cunning folk" or "wise women" who survived the persecutions of the European and North American witch crazes in the late Middle Ages and the early modern periods. These traditions lasted into and beyond the twentieth century, although today, this folk magic is practiced by only a few. For these people, spells to mend a broken heart, cure warts or other ailments, or simply to bring good luck were not, and are not, the rituals of a religion. They were, as they saw it, simply harnessing the natural powers of the world around them.

A different form of magic is that where spirits and ultimately gods are invoked in the process of rituals. Here, the magic is an integral part of a religious system, where the participants have a coherent set of beliefs that seek to explain humanity's place in the world. This kind of magic is closely related to that practiced by most modern witches—those who are part of the Wicca or Witchcraft religion. These witches point out that such magic is not "supernatural," it is simply using hidden laws of nature. However, the rituals are in the context of worshipping or revering goddesses and gods, who are in turn but many different aspects of the one true Deity.

At the heart of this belief system is the role of the Goddess, Mother Nature, or, as she is also known, the Lady.

Many of the old gods revered today by modern witches have their origins in the cultures of the Near and Middle East, where goddesses,

^ A woodcut showing witches dancing in a forest from
The Witch of the Woodlands (1655) by Lawrence Price,
a writer of pamphlets and amusing poems of the time.

∧ This engraving of *Allegory of Mother Earth* (*c*.1515) by
Italian artist Christofano Robetta depicts the Earth
as a fertile goddess at the centre of Nature.

gods, and magicians were at the heart of societies. The gods and witches of the Sumerians, Babylonians, and Egyptians in turn influenced the Hebrew world and its view of magic and gods. The shifting view of magic through this crucial period in history has profoundly affected the way that the Western world views witchcraft. When people today confront the reality of witchcraft, they are doing so with assumptions that go back thousands of years.

The Idea of the Goddess

The notion of a Mother Goddess was central to many ancient cultures, and is at the spiritual heart of the modern mystical religion of Witchcraft. But it has also been deeply controversial among historians and anthropologists. From the nineteenth century onwards, there was a growing consensus among experts that a religion worshipping the Earth Mother (or Great Goddess) had preceded all other deity-based systems of belief. At the time there was said to be a matriarchal society. Only later, the theory goes, did society become more patriarchal and the reverence for the Goddess was supplanted by a more masculine god, such as the God of the Hebrews and later the Christians.

This view of the Goddess as Mother Deity was expressed powerfully in a second-century novel known as *The Golden Ass*, written by the poet and philosopher Lucius Apuleius. In this work the goddess Isis is seen as all-embracing, all-encompassing, telling the hero, "From me come all gods and goddesses who exist."

In 1948 the British poet Robert Graves followed other nineteenth- and twentieth-century writers when he published *The White Goddess*. In this book Graves, too, suggested that there had been a pre-existing universal moon and earth Goddess.

Nowadays, however, the accepted view of most experts is that there is no evidence for a predating religion of the Goddess. The archeological and anthropological evidence suggests that societies began with small, local deities, some of whom were later subsumed into bigger, more powerful gods and goddesses.

Mother Goddess

This does not mean, though, that the Goddess did not play a central role in many ancient religions. As we saw from Apuleius in his depiction of Isis, the Goddess in the ancient world could be an immensely powerful, awesome deity, representing the moon, the earth, fertility, and nature as well as magic. What is clear is that from the beginning of the early Christian era—and possibly earlier—the worship of the Goddess was replaced during the intensely patriarchal society that developed. This eclipse of the Mother Goddess in Western culture—some would probably see it as a suppression—lasted until a revival of interest in the female deity and Nature emerged in the literary and philosophical Romantic movement of the nineteenth century. It now finds religious expression in modern Wicca.

The echoes of the Goddess did not disappear altogether, however, even from the ruthlessly dogmatic Christian Church. For, in the elevation of the Virgin Mary in Christian mythology, we see some strong similarities to the Goddess deities of the past. Though Christian scholars have insisted that she is just human, it's a point that has perhaps been lost on the millions who have prayed to her over the centuries for comfort and guidance. To them, she performs some of the roles of a Goddess.

One more aspect of the Goddess needs to be mentioned here. Modern Wiccans revere three aspects of the Goddess, the so-called Triple Goddess. These are the Maiden (or Virgin), the Mother, and the Crone (or Hag). All are seen as equally important. The Maiden is associated with spring, the waxing moon, and independence; the Mother with summer, the full moon, and creation; the Crone is associated with the growing darkness

∧ An engraving of Madonna and Child from c.1512–16 by
   Marcantonio Raimondi, designed by the artist Raphael,
   with whom he often collaborated.

∧ An image of the Babylonian goddess, Ishtar, who was
the goddess of fertility, creator of life but also associated
with the Underworld and the endless cycle of life.

of autumn, the waning moon, and wisdom. Different goddesses of the ancient world were associated with some or all of these. However, the Crone aspect, which is supposed to represent the necessary introversion and fallowness of darkness and winter as a precursor to creation, has often been represented or misrepresented as dangerous and evil. This, in turn, helped color the way that many in the ancient world regarded witchcraft. In time, the Christian world was to use this image of the elderly, female crone as part of its demonization of witchcraft.

Goddesses, Witches, and Satan

The Sumerians—whose civilization flourished from around the fourth millennium B.C. in what is today modern Iraq—and the later Babylonians had a fairly bleak view of the world around them. For them the world was full of spirits, many of them bad. As a result, each person needed his or her own personal deity for protection from attack. One of the most ferocious of the bad spirits was Lilitu, a fierce, barren, female demon who sported wings and talons on her feet and hands and prowled the night skies hunting for victims. These were usually sleeping men, and she either seduced them or sucked their blood. Also known as Ardat Lili, Lilitu uttered terrible shrieks as she flew the skies, often accompanied by owls and lions. Though Lilitu was a spirit—and thus not human—her horrible traits were ascribed by later Western culture to the "demonic" witches of the late Middle Ages and beyond.

In the Sumerian and Babylonian societies magic was widespread— the population used charms, fortune-tellers, diviners, necromancy, and oracles. Witches could be hired to put curses on others or to lift bad spells. It was in this reputedly decadent society that female witches became associated with prostitution, through the presence of hierodules, or temple (sacred) prostitutes. This association between witches and what they saw as loose morals developed in Hebrew society and beyond.

The Babylonian goddess Ishtar was the great Mother Goddess, who represented fertility and was the creator of life, and also protected men against evil. But Ishtar also represented the Underworld, and thus was connected to the endless cycle of birth, death, and the rebirth of life. As is common with many ancient goddesses, Ishtar was both lover and sister to the same god—in her case Tammuz. The legend is that when Ishtar descended into the underworld to rescue Tammuz, her "death" there resulted in the end of growth and fertility—which resumed only when the god Enki was prevailed upon to send Plant and Water to save her, and Ishtar was restored. This clearly reflects her role as goddess of both life and death, and the endless cycle of life.

In Egypt, magic was part of the society's religious view of the world and people's interaction with the gods. They saw the universe as a whole and interconnected, not divided between the natural and the supernatural. In this society, the magician and witch had an important and respected role. The great goddess Isis, one of the most powerful and important goddesses in the ancient world, was herself revered as a great practitioner of magic.

The story goes that she had been a mortal magician until she acquired the immortality of the gods by tricking the great sun god Ra into revealing his secret name. Isis achieved this by collecting some of his spit and turning it into a venomous snake. This serpent was left in Ra's path and bit him; causing the great sun god unutterable pain. The resourceful Isis was called to help the suffering Ra. At first Isis used all the other names by which Ra was known to mankind, such as Khepera and Atum, but to no avail. Eventually, she suggested that if Ra gave her his secret name, the name that had not been uttered since the start of creation, she could use its great healing power to remove the snake's venom. Ra finally agreed, and Isis healed him—at the same time becoming an immortal and powerful goddess, known as She of the Many Names.

Osiris was the husband and brother of Isis. According to legend, Osiris was killed and dismembered by his brother Seth (or Set). Isis used

∧ An engraved illustration depicting Isis, Osiris, and Horus,
published in 1873 in the first French popular illustrated
magazine *Le Magasin pittoresque*.

∧ A depiction of the goddess Isis from *Notae in Jacobi
Gaffarelli Curiositates* (1676). She has one foot in the sea
and the other on land, and the crescent Moon marks her
private parts, to show her rule over birth and creation.

her great magic to find the scattered parts of his body and bring Osiris back to life briefly, before he disappeared back to rule the Underworld. Meanwhile, Isis had a son, Horus, whom she hid and protected from Seth until he was old enough to defend himself.

These attributes of Isis give some idea of why she was so greatly worshipped and loved throughout not just Egypt but, in later centuries, much of the ancient world. Isis was a loyal partner, a strong and protective mother, a healer, and great worker of magic. Her name meant "throne" or "seat," and as the mother of Horus she was seen, by extension, as mother of the pharaohs. The goddess has also been represented suckling her son Horus, an image that bears some comparison to the later Christian depiction of the Virgin Mary and the baby Jesus. And, like Isis, Mary was also to be described as the "Queen of Heaven" by later Christians. This is not to suggest that Mary was a later aspect of Isis, but that the devotion heaped upon Mary shows she may have performed, in a restricted way, some of the functions of this goddess in an otherwise very male Christian theology.

The Witch of Endor

The Hebrew view of witchcraft was more negative, and through the translation of the Hebrew Bible into Greek, Latin, and ultimately English and other vernacular tongues, this was to have a huge impact on later Western approaches toward witches and witchcraft.

The best-known witch story of the Old Testament, the "Witch of Endor" from 1 Samuel, is a misleading translation. The word "witch" is used in English versions when the Hebrew writer was really referring to a seer or woman who divined the future. In the story itself, set in the eleventh century B.C., King Saul of Israel is terrified of a forthcoming battle with an army of Philistines, and feels abandoned by God. In desperation he goes in disguise to see the "witch" to help him know the future.

At Saul's request, the woman calls up the spirit of the dead prophet Samuel. The prophet, who seems unhappy at being disturbed, confirms that the king has indeed been deserted by God. He then predicts that Saul and his sons will die the next day after defeat at the hands of the Philistines. The prediction proves correct: Saul's three sons are killed by the Philistines and the wounded king eventually takes his own life.

In later times, many Christians thought that the conjured spirit could not have been Samuel, and was therefore the work of the Devil, showing that from the interpretation of an apparently straightforward story, Christians came to regard anyone practicing witchcraft as being in league with the diabolical.

King Solomon the Magician

While in Hebrew society, people such as mystics, seers, and necromancers were regarded with some mistrust, one of the greatest magicians or witches of all time was himself King of Israel—Solomon, son of David.

Solomon is said to have commanded a legion of devils to help build his famous and fabulous temple, in which he housed the Ark of the Covenant. His power over the demons apparently came from a magic ring, given to Solomon by God himself via an angel.

Such was Solomon's reputation as a magician that he is credited with writing the greatest of the grimoires (books of magical spells and rituals) known as the Key of Solomon. However, though its origins stretch back many centuries, there is no evidence that he wrote such a book.

Solomon reputedly had many wives—700 in all—and the small matter of 300 concubines. Solomon allowed these mostly foreign partners to worship their own gods. And Solomon himself, according to 1 Kings 11, also worshipped some of them. It is interesting that Solomon had been given great wisdom by one god and chose to use it, in part, to worship others from an even older tradition.

∧ A nineteenth-century engraving of the Witch of Endor,
by John Kay.

∧ The Sumerian demon known as Lilitu was also known as Lilith in Hebrew culture and was depicted as a dangerous demon of the night who preyed on newborn babies.

Lilith

As we have seen, the Sumerians had a demon known as Lilitu. The equivalent in Hebrew culture was Lilith. She, too, was depicted as a demon of the night, flying out to strangle or kidnap newborn children or sleeping with men to produce demonic children.

Lilith is reputed to have been the first wife of Adam, the two of them having been physically joined as twins. However, the couple, once created, soon fell out. Adam insisted that during sex she lie underneath him. Lilith demanded her equal rights, and, when Adam refused, Lilith went off in anger and gave birth to children from demons. God sent three angels after her, and they caught up with her at the Red Sea, but she refused to go back. Her punishment was that every day she would lose 100 of the demon children that she produced. Lilith's reaction to her punishment was to wage war against newborns, though she could be warded off by amulets bearing the names of the three angels who pursued her—Sansanvi, Semangelaf, and Sanvi.

In the Zohar, which is the main source of the Jewish mystical tradition the Kabbalah, it is said that Lilith's greatest power is when the moon is waning. This quality associates her with the Crone aspect of the Goddess referred to earlier, the dark side. The negative qualities given to Lilith were later connected with the Middle Ages concept of the diabolical witch.

Lilith has been championed as an important mythological character by some feminists, who see in her refusal to comply with Adam's demands and subsequent punishment a parable of how a patriarchal society suppressed women.

One more mystical interpretation of the Lilith/Adam story, and one that also feeds into modern witchcraft, is that Lilith represents the wild, passionate subconscious side of the human spirit. Adam represents civilization, trying—and failing—to control this wild subconscious. The two are set in opposition. In this interpretation, modern witchcraft is trying to bring these two elements into harmony and balance.

Satan

Western culture is now familiar with the idea of the Devil, the negative counterpart to the one true God, who tried to turn humanity away from the path of righteousness. However, not all religions and cultures developed this idea, and in quite this way.

Many religions had one deity, or series of deities, who collectively represented both light and darkness. Good and bad were rolled into one. The development of Mazdaism, the faith based on the teachings of the Persian prophet Zoroaster (*c.* 638–553 B.C.), saw a different approach to the world. In this religion, the good god, Ahura Mazda, was in conflict with the evil god Ahriman. This Good-versus-Evil notion influenced Judaism and later had a huge influence on Christian thinking.

In the Old Testament, the development of Satan as this personification of an Evil force was gradual. "Satan," the Hebrew word for this force, simply meant "adversary" or "the obstructor." But during the age of the apocryphal and apocalyptic writings from around 200 B.C. to A.D. 150, the Devil in Judaism became a tangible figure of the dark, set in opposition to the light and to God. He was, to them, a fallen angel.

During this period of apocalyptic writings, Christianity developed its own traditions and beliefs. The idea of the Devil functioned as a counterbalance to Christ. Christ was here to save you from the Devil. It was the ultimate Good versus the ultimate Evil.

This philosophy had implications for witches and witchcraft: You could not order an angel to perform a task or grant a wish; you could only pray to it. Therefore, those people (witches) who did invoke spirits were by definition calling up bad spirits. Since these bad spirits were obviously being controlled by the Devil, then anyone calling up the spirits was in league with the Devil. This reasoning was the background to much of the Christian-inspired persecution of witches in later Western culture and is still quite prevalent today among many Christian fundamentalists.

∧ A depiction of an amulet for protection against Lilith, from the
Sefer Raziel (Book of Raziel the Angel), a medieval Kabbalah
grimoire. This would have been worn round the necks of pregnant
women or placed in the rooms where newborns slept.

POWERFUL

Witchcraft and magic were central to the lives of many Greeks. One of their great gods, the revered and feared Hecate, was the goddess of witchcraft.

GODDESSES,

POWERFUL

Yet in later periods, the Greeks described witches in dark, more sinister terms, which had an influence on how both the Romans and later Western culture viewed witchcraft.

WITCHES

The Magic of the Greeks

Greek culture was very literate and was to have a profound influence on the way that Western society developed. Mathematics, geometry, algebra, natural sciences, philosophy, and drama are just some of the areas in which the Greeks bequeathed a powerful legacy to the West. It is no wonder, therefore, that Greek thought has shaped our modern ideas about witchcraft.

It is true the Greeks did not quite see witches in the way the panic-stricken persecutors of the late Middle Ages saw them: with their broomsticks, flying ointments, satanic rituals, and mocking of the One True Faith. These were later embellishments and were essentially Christian in origin. But the Greeks did develop an image of witches that saw them as mostly female, dangerous, unconventional, highly sexual, and alien. They were capable of acts of great evil. At the same time, though, witches could also be seen in more positive terms: as beautiful, powerful, loyal, and able to perform acts of great love and kindness.

This complexity of view was also mirrored in the way ancient Greece regarded magic. There were perhaps three or four main strands of magical practice that we can identify in their society.

The first was the highest form of magic, which they themselves called *theourgia*, from *theos* meaning a god and *ergon* meaning work. Literally translated, it means "work relating to the gods." This referred to so-called high, ritualistic magic in which the person involved (maybe a priest) sought to raise his or her consciousness to the point where it met with the divine. It is very close in concept of working with the Goddess that is at the heart of modern pagan witchcraft.

A second form of magic was that employed by the civic state, in the form of consulting oracles (for example at Delphi), augury (the telling of the future from the flight patterns of birds), or the reading of entrails.

This distinguishes it from a third category, that which might be called "popular" magic. This in itself could be split into two categories: *mageia*,

∧ This seventeenth-century etching depicts a scene from
Homer's *Odyssey*: the Greek goddess and witch, Circe,
sits with books and wand, and the men she has
transformed into animals.

< In this 1685 engraving by Johan Wilhelm Baur, Medea rejuvenates her husband Jason's aged father, Aeson, by draining his blood, so that she can replace it with a special herbal brew of her own. Aeson lies within a witches' circle, naked, while Medea stands over him alongside a steaming cauldron with two winged demon figures above.

which is closer to the modern sense of "sorcery" and was practiced by a magician or *magos* (magus); and *goetia*, practiced by *goetes*.

The *magi*, for want of a better term, could be described as professional magicians who were often hired by the great and the good to carry out magical work on their behalf. The popularity of such magicians suggests that many of them were held in high esteem in Greek society.

The picture, though, is blurred. The ruling male elites tended to regard all magic (other than that state-sanctioned form or *theourgia*) with suspicion. Magic could be a threat to the social order. Magic was often associated with those outside this elite—women, low-born men, and, of course, foreigners. Meanwhile, most of the people who wrote at this time and whose work has survived were members of the same elite. So we possibly get a distorted view of how "ordinary" Greeks regarded magic and witchcraft. That said, the words of the philosopher Plato, who dismissed such professional magicians as "charlatan priests of foreign divinities," probably summed up the view of others of his social class and standing.

The last form of magic, *goetia*, was apparently associated with charlatans and deception. The *goetes* were peddlers of potions, love spells, healing herbs, and curses. Some of them might have been genuine, some of them undoubtedly not.

Daimones or Demons?

In earlier Greek times, in the age of Homer, the word *daimon* was used almost as another word for god. It certainly had few, if any, negative associations. In later years the *daimones* came to be seen as morally neutral. They were spirits, intermediaries between humans and the gods, and had powers, including that of prophecy.

After Plato, it was considered that there could be both good and evil demons, spirits with some of the qualities and failings of humans.

∧ The Greek goddess of hunting, Artemis, was also believed
to be a goddess of childbirth. She was also identified
with the Egyptian goddess, Isis.

∧ Seventeenth-century engraving of the goddess Hecate, shown as three-formed, which is often interpreted as connected with the appearance of the full moon, half moon, and new moon.

By the time of later Greek thought, *daimones* had become primarily linked with evil, a view that helped shape the concept in Judaism and then early Christianity. Gone was the idea that there was both good and bad in demons—the angels were on the side of God; the demons were placed firmly in the other camp with the Devil. Anyone who invoked, consulted, summoned, or was in any way magically involved with the demons was thus automatically on the "wrong" side.

The Great Goddess

The Greeks are rightly well known for their extraordinary variety of gods. Among these, one of the greatest, most powerful, most loved—and most feared—was Hecate.

Hecate, whose name means "One Who Stands Aloof," was and remains one of the most complex of all goddesses. She predates Greek deities, but was adopted by the Greeks and was revered even by the father of the gods, Zeus himself. Hecate has many roles. She is at once the goddess of fertility, the goddess of the moon, and the goddess of the Underworld. Hecate is also the goddess of all magic and witchcraft. It is in the last roles that Hecate has become notorious in Western culture, in which she has been portrayed roaming the night with red-eyed hounds from Hell, haunting graveyards, provoking dogs to howl with terror at her unseen presence, causing nightmares and insanity. To Shakespeare, in his play *Macbeth*, she is the feared Queen of the Witches. One of her ancient names was The Nameless One.

Yet Hecate is far from being a one-dimensional character, either in Greek thought or in modern interpretations of her. She is often depicted with three heads and even three bodies, emphasizing her ability to see into both the past and the future, and also her role as goddess of crossroads. Indeed, those who worshipped her are said to have left offerings for her at crossroads. Crossroads have a symbolic as well as a literal function:

They are in between one path and another; they show transition, and in the context of Hecate are connected with the transition points of birth and death. Once again in the ancient world, life and death, light and dark, are linked as part of the whole. Death cannot be without life, and life cannot be without death—the endless cycle. Hecate, too, is linked with childbirth and with midwives. This is a significant connection: In the Middle Ages midwives were sometimes persecuted as witches.

Hecate was also a moon goddess, sometimes linked with the other goddesses Selene and Artemis, in which she, Hecate, was the waning, dark side of the moon. For others, though, she was the moon—its waxing, waning, and fullness all in one. In a modern interpretation of her, Hecate is wisdom, our subconscious, the inner, hidden self—the dark side that we have to unite with the conscious mind in order to achieve unity in our lives.

The main role of Hecate in one of the Greek myths emphasizes many of her distinctive characteristics. It is she who helped search for Persephone after the latter was abducted from a peaceful, sunlit meadow by the brooding lord of the Underworld, Hades. As a result, Persephone spends part of the year traveling to the earth to stay (which brings spring and summer) and part of the year descending back to Hell for a period (autumn and winter). Her companion is Hecate, linking the goddess to the seasonal cycle.

Pan

Pan, the half-man, half-goat son of Hermes, was an important god, symbolizing nature, lust, playfulness, and all things pastoral. He is now identified in modern witchcraft as a version of the Horned God. The Horned God is seen as a consort to the Goddess, and his annual birth at Yuletide and his symbolic death at the end of each summer mark the passing of the seasons, the cycle of birth, death, and rebirth in nature.

∧ An eighteenth-century engraving of the Greek god Pan,
depicting his half-human and half-goat form, which was
later associated with the Devil by the Christian Church.

∧ A woodcut from an illustrated edition of Ovid's *Metamorphoses* published in 1563, showing the sorceress Circe turning Odysseus' men into pigs.

Some of the physical characteristics of Pan, including his goatlike appearance and sexual appetite, were later attributed in the Christian world to the Devil. Because of his liberated and uninhibited behavior, Pan is regarded by witches as the antithesis of the moralizing and rule-driven Christian Church.

Circe

Circe, sometimes described as the daughter of Hecate and sometimes as the child of Helios and Perse, plays an important role in Homer's *Odyssey*. When Odysseus and his men chance upon her doleful island of Aeaea, she turns his men into pigs, but Odysseus, with the help of the god Hermes and the herb moly, escapes this fate; eventually he and Circe spend a happy year together on the island. She later helps him on his voyage home.

The image of Circe is complicated. She is depicted as a beautiful woman, a goddess, a witch, or a sorceress, someone who has no qualms about turning men into animals; but equally she is prepared to help another for no obvious ulterior motive. Certainly she had a powerful reputation as a worker of magic: Homer calls her "Circe of the Braided Tresses" because she is said to have been able to use her braids to control the forces of nature. Knots are commonly used in magical spells. She was also an early example of the link between witchcraft and herbs.

Medea the Vengeful

The image of Circe has a certain moral ambivalence attached to it, but the great Greek witch Medea is depicted as a darker character still. Sometimes described as the niece of Circe, and a priestess of Hecate, Medea developed a reputation in mythology for dealing brutally with anyone who crossed her. The daughter of Aeëtes, the King of Colchis, Medea helped Jason and his famous Argonauts to retrieve the equally famous Golden Fleece. The witch falls hopelessly in love with Jason, and, when they are later pursued by Aeëtes, Medea kills and then dismembers her own brother Absyrtus, knowing that the king will have to stop to bury and honor his dead son.

Later, after she and Jason have happily spent years together, she is distraught that he falls for another woman, named Creusa. The witch sends her rival a garment that bursts into flames as she puts it on, killing Creusa and destroying the palace she lives in. As further revenge on Jason, Medea then kills their two sons.

This portrayal of Medea by a succession of ancient writers contains some elements that were later to be reinforced onto medieval witches—sexual passion, jealousy, a ruthless wickedness, and the slaughter of children. Through Medea, the terrible revenge and passionate jealousy of a woman scorned became the attributes of a witch.

Medea was a powerful witch, known as the "wise one," who could do, and did, magic for good as well as bad; and she was eventually, according to legend, made immortal and became the wife of one of the great Greek heroes, Achilles. It is, however, her vengeful, consuming jealousy—a gift for writers of tragedy—that has survived as her enduring image. And the image of the witch, too.

Other witches from Greek legend give an impression of their power. The Witches of Thessaly, for example, were followers of Hecate. They were said to be so powerful in their craft that they could "draw down the moon" from the sky and use it in their magic. The ritual of "Drawing Down the Moon" is now an important part of modern witchcraft, in which the high priestess draws down the moon—representing the Goddess—into her body and so "becomes" the Goddess.

∧ An engraving from a 1606 Italian edition of Ovid's *Metamorphoses*, depicting a vengeful Medea destroying Jason's family and home.

ORIGINS OF WITCHCRAFT

Since the dawn of time, humans have sought to understand the links between people and nature, to discern the causes of events, and to explore the mysteries of birth, life, and death. These aims eventually led to the practices of witchcraft that may be called simple folk magic or sorcery.

Inevitably, this magic was intimately involved with nature: The earth, wind, water, and fire were crucial to early humans, as were the rising and setting of the sun, the waxing and waning of the moon, and the passing of the seasons and the animals and plants that came and went with them. Early humans had to utilize these forces and these secrets evolved into religion and magic.

Within most societies magic and religion have indeed been closely associated with each other. In one sense the use of prayer is simply a form of magic—using one's will to achieve change in the material world with the aid of divine intervention.

The practice of community rituals, to ensure, for example, that good crops spring from the earth in the coming year, is linked with the specific belief that there is something or someone out there who can help make this happen. Such sorcery is then regarded as a positive influence.

However, when this kind of magic is practiced in secret, then it falls outside that culture's rules. Thus, societies have always tended to have an ambivalent attitude toward sorcery and witchcraft. Witchcraft is all right as long as it's performed according to our rules and expectations.

———————✳———————

Witchcraft and Shamanism

One ancient form of healing and divination is shamanism, a practice that has survived in some cultures—notably parts of Asia, North America, and Northern Europe—to this day. The essence of shamanism is that the shaman enters a trancelike state in which, through communication with spirits, he or she can use powers to heal or to foresee the future. There are strong similarities between shamanism and modern witchcraft, and many witches incorporate specifically shamanistic practices into their rituals.

MAGIC AND THE BIRTH OF CHRISTIANITY

The Roman goddess Diana is one of the most important figures in witchcraft, and has greatly influenced the feminist view of the Wiccan religion. But Rome also feared witchcraft as socially subversive. Meanwhile, the emergence of Christianity spelled doom for the pagan beliefs that had stood at the heart of the Greco-Roman world for hundreds of years.

Diana the Goddess

The Roman Empire occupies an important place in the history of witchcraft. Such was its wide-ranging dominance that it provided a bridge from the ancient world, the world of the Sumerians, Egyptians, Persians, Babylonians, and Greeks, into the Christian era in Europe.

The Romans were generally suspicious of witchcraft and magic: for them, it was just another subversive element in a world where order always seemed to be under attack from chaos. Yet the Romans also bequeathed us the legacy of one of the most powerful goddesses of the ancient world, a goddess who was to have a huge influence on the development of the modern witchcraft religion.

Diana/Artemis

There is little doubt that, of all the goddesses associated with witchcraft, Diana stands out as the most important. In the Greek world she was known as Artemis, and she was also identified with the Egyptian goddess Isis. Yet it is under her Roman guise that Diana is best known and most worshipped; it is certainly the name by which she is generally revered by modern witches. In fact, this goddess has given her name to the Dianic tradition of modern Wicca, a tradition that grew out of the feminist movement in the United States in the 1970s (see pages 212–26).

It is not difficult to see why Diana appeals to many women in witchcraft. She is the Maiden Goddess, independent, free-spirited, and beholden to no one, including any man. Diana is a moon goddess, who exemplifies the waxing of the moon, an important time in witchcraft for carrying out magic rituals. For some she represents the moon in its entirety.

The headstrong daughter of Jupiter/Zeus and the twin of Apollo, Diana/Artemis was also strongly identified with childbirth. Her mother,

∧ Engraving of Correggio's fresco of Diana (c.1519), the
Roman goddess of the hunt. Also known as Artemis,
she is particularly revered by modern-day witches.

∧ Depicted in this sixteenth-century woodcut with a bow
and arrow, and a fierce hunting dog, Diana was fierce,
independent, and not beholden to any man.

Leto, was said to have suffered great pain in giving birth to her twin Apollo, and Artemis helped ease that suffering by acting as midwife. Thus women have traditionally offered prayers to Artemis or Diana to help soothe their pain in childbirth.

Goddess of the Hunt

Diana has a fierce and aggressive side to her character, as shown by her well-known portrayal as a goddess of the hunt. The story goes that, while still young, Diana displayed such a love of the wild that her father gave her a bow and arrow and a pack of hunting hounds so she could run through the wilderness, able to look after herself and to protect others. This is another important aspect of the goddess Diana: she is closely identified with helping out those who needed protection, both animals and humans, and in particular with helping those women who had been brutalized by men.

It is also significant that Diana, who in one guise was known as Lady of Wild Things, is associated with nature and the countryside, as modern witchcraft identifies itself very strongly with all things natural.

In the early years of Christianity, there was perhaps some ambivalence toward Diana among some of its followers. This is hinted at in excavations near the site of the once-fabulous ancient temple dedicated to her at Ephesus (now in modern Turkey), which was sacked by the Goths in the third century A.D. (This vast temple was one of the Seven Wonders of the World.) The discoveries apparently included a pit where Christians had broken and discarded many statues of the old pagan gods they despised. Two statues of Diana survived intact, however. This has prompted speculation that the statues were spared because some early Christians saw links between the virgin goddess Diana and the Virgin Mary, the mother of Jesus. Whether this is true or not, Mary is certainly supposed to have lived (and possibly died) in Ephesus, and even now there is a house and a church dedicated to her there. It is interesting how legends of the virgin "Mother of God" become entangled with those of ancient goddesses such as Diana and also Isis. One of the strengths of the Christian Church—and one of the reasons for its spread across different cultures—has been its ability to assimilate other beliefs and icons.

Linked to Diana is the rather confusing story of Aradia. Aradia is the leading character of the book *Aradia: Gospel of the Witches*, published by the American folklorist Charles Leland in 1899. Leland claimed the story came from a witch called Maddalena, whom he met in Italy and who supposedly provided him with stories and traditions from what she claimed was a surviving witch cult associated with Diana. According to this story, Diana was known as the Queen of the Witches, and Aradia was her daughter. Diana sent Aradia to earth to teach the secrets of witchcraft to the poor and the oppressed, so that they might fight against their rulers. Few people now take seriously Leland's (or Maddalena's) claims that there was any surviving witch cult, based on Diana or anyone else.

The importance of Aradia, however, is that she is often worshipped as an aspect of the Goddess by modern Wiccans. The name Aradia is derived from Herodias, the wife of King Herod in the New Testament, whose own name was at times linked with Diana.

Bacchus

Another important religious aspect to come out of the Roman Empire was the rites of the Bacchanalia, the orgiastic activities of the followers of the god Bacchus. The key characteristics of these rites included secret meetings at night, initiation rituals, torchlit meetings held in caves, excessive eating and drinking, and wild, untamed sex. Their importance to the history of witchcraft is that these powerful images, painted by

∧ Bacchus was the Roman god of the grape harvest,
   winemaking and wine, of ritual madness and ecstasy.

^ A detail of the witch Erichtho from a painting by John Hamilton Mortimer (1740–79) entitled *Sextus Pompeius consulting Erichtho before the Battle of Pharsalia.*

contemporary writers such as Livy, were to influence later European thought about witches. As the historian Professor Jeffrey B. Russell has written, "The historian Livy's description of the Bacchanalia became an important part of the literary tradition of European witchcraft."

The Roman Witch

Alongside Livy's depiction of the Bacchanalia—whose accuracy we can only guess at—other Roman writers painted a generally dark picture of witches. In his writing on Medea, the Roman Ovid seems determined to portray her as an outsider. Her hair is long and unkempt, her clothes loose and disordered, she shrieks and yells, while all around the natural world is silent. Another writer, Lucan, describes a witch called Erichtho as old and very ugly, a hag who rifles graveyards and the corpses of the recently dead for body parts to use in her grim rituals. Her feet instantly destroy the fertility of any land they touch.

Such lurid depictions of witches as old, ugly, and barren—and female—were stereotypes that survived well into the later Christian era; and were very familiar to the educated classes of those times.

Poison, Laws, and Emperors

The Romans feared witchcraft and magic. That is to say, the Roman elites feared magic because they felt vulnerable to it. Even if you were a powerful senator or an almighty emperor, you could still fall victim to attack from evil spells.

As early as 450 B.C., the Romans had laws against what they called *veneficia*, or acts of harmful magic. These included evil charms or incantations against people, or using magic to spirit fruit or vegetables away from someone else's crop and into one's own. More dramatically still, there were two mass persecutions of people using magic during 184–183 B.C. and 180–179 B.C., when possibly as many as 5,000 people in all were executed for using harmful magic.

This was followed in 81 B.C. with the *lex Cornelia de sicariis et veneficis* (Sulla's Law dealing with Murder and Acts of Poisoning), which was aimed primarily at poisoning, but came to include magical rituals involving herbs. Then, in 33 B.C., hundreds if not thousands of astrologers and necromancers were expelled from Rome.

Later still, the first Roman emperor, Augustus (27 B.C.–A.D. 14), ordered that some 2,000 books of magical spells or grimoires should be collected and burned, in case their magic should be used against him.

Such measures show that the Roman state was fearful of those things it felt it could not control. It must be remembered that these events were well before the Christian era. Rome encouraged or tolerated belief in a variety of pagan gods and magical rituals in the context of state-sanctioned faiths. With their lavish temples and wealthy and powerful adherents, such religions could be accepted. The distinction is similar to that made by the Greeks, who happily embraced those who practiced *theourgia* or divine magic—magic that was effectively part of a mystery religion.

What could not be tolerated in such a centralized society were individuals or small groups who did not fit into the system, and who in particular were suspected of causing harm by witchcraft. Such threats, when identified, were therefore met with ruthless repression. It was a pattern that would be repeated with even more force in Europe well over a thousand years later. There was a crucial difference, however. It was not alternative belief systems that the Romans feared, but the very real danger, as they saw it, of practical magic and subversives. In contrast, the later Christian elite, while also determined to maintain power and status, added a new factor into the equation of their persecution of witches—religious dogma.

∧ This first-century B.C. mosaic at the Villa of Cicero in Pompeii depicts a scene from a comedy play, in which two women sit in consultation with a witch.

^ This nineteenth-century engraving illustrates the
conversion of Constantine I to Christianity in A.D. 312.

Rome, Pagans, and Christianity

Until Rome adopted the Christian faith as one of its religions, Christianity had been simply another faith competing for support in the first three centuries of the first millennium A.D. It was persecuted by those in power and deeply split in different factions and beliefs. All this was to change after the emergence of Constantine as Emperor.

Constantine the Great

It was under Emperor Constantine that Christianity first acquired formal acceptance, which led quickly to the primacy of Christianity to the exclusion of all other faiths. The pagan gods, those who underpinned the beliefs of the practitioners of high magic then, and of the modern witchcraft religion now, were abruptly jettisoned.

Before winning a battle against rival Maxentius in A.D. 312, Constantine is said to have had a vision of a cross appearing in the sky, with the words in Latin, "In this sign you will be victorious." He adopted the cross as his emblem and the following year, A.D. 313, he and his co-emperor, Licinius, issued the famous Edict of Milan, which gave the Christian religion lawful status in the empire.

A little more than half a century after Constantine's reign, the official faith of the empire was Christian. The statutes, buildings, and writings relating to pagan worship were destroyed, and pagan worshippers were persecuted, notably under the emperors Valens and Theodosius. The latter outlawed pagan worship in A.D. 392. For those who practiced magic the situation was worse still. Under pre-Christian Roman law those who used magic to harm others—or were suspected of doing so—could be executed. Under the Christian emperors, however, anyone who practiced magic could face execution. For witches, the Roman Empire had often been a difficult and dangerous place. The future now looked even bleaker.

EUROPEAN

Magic and witchcraft also flourished outside the so-called classical civilizations of Greece and Rome, among the Germanic, Norse, and Celtic peoples.

AND NORTHERN

The gods of the north, and especially the Celtic deities, have had a huge influence on modern witchcraft. They have also helped spawn many well-known legends such as King Arthur, the Green Man, and Robin Hood.

WITCHCRAFT

Early European Magic

We have already seen the importance of the classical civilizations of Greece and Rome in the history of witchcraft. However, the rest of Europe has an equally important place in the story. It was in Europe, in the lands occupied by the Celts, the Germanic tribes, and later the Norsemen, that people worshipped many of the old gods and goddesses—a worship that exists today. In particular, much of modern Wicca looks backward toward the Celts for its inspiration—for the Celtic association with nature and magical traditions.

The Celts in History

The story of the Celts, in particular, needs to be approached with some caution. One of the curious things about the Celts is that, the more they are studied, the less we seem to know about them. In some cases, we actually know more about the people who preceded them than we do about the Celts themselves. Part of the reason for this is that they had little or no written tradition. Another is that their religious beliefs clearly did not rely on the building of structures in the way that other cultures have done.

This means that we get much of our information about the Celts from incomplete archeological remains, and the testimony of contemporary Greek and Roman writers who either had little interest in the Celts or were intent on portraying them in a particular light for social or political reasons. Another source of information on the Celts are the writings of later Christians in Europe who, again, either may not have understood the Celtic traditions, or may have deliberately misrepresented them and their non-Christian beliefs. What follows is an attempt to explain what we do—and what we don't—know about the Celts and their deities.

∧ "The Druid Grove," taken from an 1845 book *Old England: A Pictoral Museum* by Charles Knight. This scene shows a bearded and robed man sitting in the shade of a giant tree; in the background a group of three robed figures surrounds a smaller tree.

∧ Taken from a second-century Roman monument, a Druid
carries the crescent of the Sixth Day of the Moon.

Druids

The tradition of magic in Celtic times is closely connected with one of the most fascinating groups of people from European history, namely the Druids. The modern revival of interest in Druidism means that we are all familiar with the image of people in long, flowing robes holding ceremonies at significant points of the year, most notably midsummer.

Yet little detail is known about Druid practices, their beliefs, or about the gods they worshipped. This is partly because the Druids used an oral tradition to pass knowledge on from one generation to the next. It is said that the training of a Druid could take up to twenty years; that they valued the use of the spoken word because it utilized the power of the mind rather than having to rely on written-down information. Whatever the reason, it seems that the bulk of their knowledge died with them.

What we do know about the Druids suggests that they were intermediaries between the Celtic peoples and their gods and held immense power in society.

The magic of the Druids seems to have been highly ritualistic, and concerned with such matters as people who could change shape, divination, and casting spells to harm or kill people and to influence the weather. It is thought that most of their magic and religious rituals were performed during the day and often in sacred oak groves. The Druids have often been linked with the oak tree, symbolizing nature and the wisdom of the earth.

One of the main roles of a Druid was as the spiritual and magical adviser to the king of a tribe. They also had the function of teacher, healer, and judge. It appears that Druids were almost exclusively male, though some classical writers do record women performing similar roles.

The Druids, then, give us a glimpse of sacred Celtic society, albeit a hazy one. With their steady demise under the Romans and then Christians, a whole magical tradition appears to have been lost from Europe.

The Seithr of the Norse

The use of magic or witchcraft was prevalent throughout the ancient Germanic or Teutonic peoples who lived in much of Northern Europe. Their practices seem quite familiar to those who know anything of the traditions of witchcraft. They involved the making of wax or dough figures, and using needles, fire, or water to inflict harm upon the person whom the figure represented.

The Visigoths in Europe meanwhile found it necessary to pass laws in the sixth century that set out the punishment for those "storm makers" who went around threatening to ruin a farmer's crops, unless he paid up the protection money. Elsewhere, Anglo-Saxon magic ranged from simple charms to remove warts to elaborate spells aimed at destroying enemies.

However, one of the best-preserved traditions of Northern Europe was the form of magic known as seithr in the Norse culture. This kind of sorcery was widespread and was described in one of our principal sources of knowledge about Norse mythology, the Edda, written by the thirteenth-century Icelandic historian Snorri Sturluson.

Seithr was carried out largely at night, and mostly by women known as volvas. In folklore they are supposed to have ridden out at night on animals such as wolves or bears, or on wooden rails, to meet other volvas—nightly meetings that were later equated by Christians with the Sabbats (seasonal festivals) of witches.

In historical terms, the real practice of seithr has been likened to that of shamanistic magic. It usually involved a woman sitting on a platform or high seat, and then attaining a trancelike state (sometimes the singing of spells or chanting was used to help induce the trance). In this state, she would answer questions, on subjects such as forecasting the weather and seasons, and predictions of love between a young couple. Sometimes seithr was associated with harmful magic, but more often with this kind of helpful divination.

∧ A woodcut from Francesco Maria Guazzo's *Compendium Maleficarum* (1608). The Devil, in the form of a flying goat, carries a witch to the Sabbat.

∧ The Norse goddess Frigg was the wife of Odin, and was associated
   with the goddesses Freya and Skadi as the Triple Goddess.

In the Icelandic work *Eiríks saga rauða* (the saga of Erik the Red), a volva was described as answering questions on the topic most concerning a community, namely the famine they were suffering. Then later, giving more personal answers to individuals about their lives.

This story gives an interesting insight into how these volvas were viewed by society; almost as a public consultation service. However, not all the accounts in Norse culture of the seers are so benign. One story of an early king of Sweden describes his being crushed to death by a sorceress who had taken the form of a horse. Another story tells of a witch who was put on trial in Iceland for riding a man to death in a similar way. But many of the stories of these traveling seers or witches are positive. This may be explained by the fact that Christianity came much later to parts of Scandinavia than most of the rest of Europe, and so the stories have less of the usual suspicion of the magical practices that is typical in subsequent Christian depictions.

The Northern Gods

The Norse goddess most associated with seithr is Freya. Freya (or Freyja) is the twin sister of Frey and was said to be the most renowned of goddesses in the Norse pantheon, as well as being very beautiful.

Freya was associated with a number of different aspects—sexual passion, magic, death, and fertility. Freya mourns her husband Od (or Odur) who appears to have died, and as she weeps for her loss, the land goes cold and barren. This represents the coming of winter. Freya goes in search of her husband and eventually finds him. They return home, whereupon the spring returns. This is a familiar story in mythology, depicting the ebb and flow of the seasons. Moreover, the idea of a mother Goddess and her male consort, who dies and then is reborn, is central to much of modern witchcraft.

Freya has also been linked with another Norse goddess, Frigg, the wife of the supreme god, Odin. Frigg, like Freya, was associated with childbirth and the two of them are sometimes seen as being two aspects of the Triple Goddess—a phenomenon already referred to in the context of Greece and Rome. The goddess Skadi, who was connected with hunting, may have made up the third aspect.

Odin himself was also closely identified with magic. The great one-eyed All-Father God—also known as Woden or Wotan in other parts of Europe—was, among other things, the god of magic. Among the many stories told about Odin is one in which he sacrificed one of his eyes in return for great wisdom and magical knowledge.

The Celtic Gods

There is little evidence that the Celts in different parts of Europe had many gods in common. A large number of their gods were localized, though there is little doubting the importance of the goddess figure to the general Celtic religious tradition.

An interesting deity in Irish Celtic mythology is the great goddess Danu, who is revered by modern witches as a Celtic mother goddess and seems to have been a major figure in the Celtic divine world. She appears as the Mother in the ancient Irish pantheon Tuatha De Danann, or "the tribes of the goddess Danu." Danu (or Anu) was associated with magic and was celebrated particularly at the festival of Beltane, on May 1.

Other important goddesses include Morrigan, a warlike deity who is often linked with other goddesses as part of the triple aspect common among many of the gods, and Rhiannon, a beautiful goddess who rode on a white horse and whose name means "divine queen."

One Celtic deity who certainly was worshipped in different parts of Europe was Lugh (or Lug), who was revered in Ireland, and also in

∧ Engraving of Odin (1883), the supreme Norse god of
wisdom and war, as well as magic.

∧ The Celtic God Cernunnos is an important figure for
Wiccans, as the consort of the Goddess.

Gaul (modern France), Spain, and Switzerland. He was regarded as a sun god in Ireland, and the important Irish (and now Wiccan) festival of Lughnasadh on August 1 is named after him. Lugh is said to have carried a magical spear and was accompanied by two ravens. In this he shows similarity to the Norse god Odin.

Ceridwen is another important Celtic figure, closely associated with witchcraft and sorcery. In an old Welsh story, Ceridwen is skilled in magic and uses her cauldron to brew up wisdom and knowledge for her son. Her servant eats the brew by accident, and after a series of chases is eventually eaten by Ceridwen. She in turn gives birth to her hugely gifted son. Ceridwen is now revered by many modern Wiccans as the goddess of wisdom, divination, and magic. She is linked to the cauldron, which has traditionally symbolized fertility and rebirth.

The Horned God

Cernunnos is one version of the Horned God, who was worshipped widely by the Celts and who is an important figure in modern witchcraft. To Wiccans, the Horned God is the consort of the Goddess. He is born at the winter solstice, when the days start to get longer, marries the Goddess at Beltane (May 1), and dies at the summer solstice, when the days begin to get shorter. Other names used include the Oak King, who is born in winter, and the Holly King, who takes over from him at midsummer.

Some of the attributes of the Horned God, notably the horns, were later used by Christians in their image of the Devil. For the Celts and for modern witches, however, the Horned God was simply a representation of the endless pattern of life, death, and rebirth.

The figure of Herne the Hunter is also linked with Cernunnos by modern pagans. Herne was reputedly the leader of the Wild Hunt, the ghostly, terrifying, nocturnal procession of the dead. This legend surfaces all over Europe, including in England, where William Shakespeare, in the play *The Merry Wives of Windsor*, refers to Herne as haunting the forest at Windsor.

Legends of Europe

A famous character of European legend who has occasionally been associated with Herne is Robin Hood. This English outlaw, who may or may not have been a real historical character, supposedly lived in the once-massive Sherwood Forest in Nottinghamshire in central England, from where he fought daily to take from the rich and give to the poor. To some, this story of the outlaw in the forest may be a metaphor for the forest-dwelling Herne, a figure discarded by Christianity, but still serving his people.

Perhaps more convincing is the link between Robin Hood and the legend of the Green Man. The Green Man is a figure found across Europe who is commonly represented as a man peering out from the foliage of a forest. It is possible to see a link between the outlaw Robin Hood and his men dressed all in green, surviving hidden in a dense wood, and that of the Green Man, himself peering out through the foliage. It has also been suggested that the Green Man is the Green Knight in the Arthurian story of Sir Gawain and the Green Knight.

The Green Man is subtly different from Herne: The latter represents the animals of the forest, the former the lush green vegetation. The Green Man's other names include Green Jack, Green George, and Jack-in-the-Green. The closeness of modern pagan witchcraft to nature and the increasing concern over the environment of the planet have made the Green Man an increasingly important figure among pagans and witches.

^ Arthurian legend is full of enduring magicians and
enchanters, such as Nimue, the 'Lady of the Lake',
here illustrated by Howard Pyle in 1903.

CONCLUSION

Legacy of the Ancient World

The practice of witchcraft was woven into the societies of the ancient world. Magic evolved separately from religion, but in some cultures, notably Egyptian and Greek, it became an important expression of theology. Nor did the ancient world always have the distinction that we see in modern times between the known and the unknowable, between science and belief. Nature, humans, the gods, and magic were all connected.

The sometimes bewildering array of deities who inhabited the ancient world was one of the most fascinating parts of those societies. Isis, Hecate, Diana, Freya, Cernunnos—they all played their parts in people's lives. But as the old societies began to crumble, so too did the armies of gods, who fell prey to the more organized and centralized monotheist religions. Within such a world of one true God and a codified set of beliefs, the practice of magic found it hard to flourish.

In a world of many gods and many spirits, some good, some bad, but none evil, the witch could exist as a feared but important conduit between humans and those gods. But once the Devil arrived as the formal enemy of the One God, magic, witchcraft, and witches were all to be associated with Evil.

The writings of Greek and particularly Roman writers such as Ovid began the now familiar portrayal of witches as old, barren, and outcast. The old societies may have been more understanding of the importance of magic and witches, but the writings and art of the ancients also developed those stereotypical images of the witch. And, when Christian societies later began to wage war on witchcraft, they found some of the ammunition in these echoes from the past.

∧ Detail of a fresco depicting the Christian persecution of the
Druids, found in the basilica of St. Boniface's Abbey, Munich.

THE WHEEL
OF THE YEAR

Modern witches divide their year into eight festivals or Sabbats. These are days when the members of a coven will gather together for a celebration. They have been described as witches' holidays.

Each Sabbat has a different ritual associated with it, according to that festival's meaning in the cycle of the year. For historical reasons, all dates and seasons refer to the Northern Hemisphere.

There are four major Sabbats—**Samhain** (October 31), **Imbolc** (February 2), **Beltane** (May 1) and **Lughnasadh/Lammas** (July 31). These correspond to four old Celtic festivals (Lammas was the Anglo-Saxon equivalent of Lughnasadh). Some witches celebrate Beltane on April 30 and Lughnasadh on August 1.

The other four lesser festivals are the two solstices and the two equinoxes: the winter solstice, spring equinox, midsummer and the autumn equinox. They are sometimes referred to as Yule, Ostara/Eostre, Litha, and Mabon.

Samhain   October 31

In the Celtic tradition this was the equivalent of New Year's Eve, symbolizing the descent into the darkness, which is essential if light and new life are to come again. It is also regarded as the time of the Lord of Misrule, a period of chaos before order is restored.

Imbolc   February 2

Sometimes referred to by its Christian name Candlemas, Imbolc symbolizes the first stirrings of growth and the new spring, and coincides with Groundhog Day. Witches often associate this festival with the Celtic goddess Brigid.

Beltane   May 1

For witches, this is the most joyous of the festivals, intimately associated with fertility and sexuality. Traditionally on this day cattle were driven between fires to purify them. Beltane honors the symbolic union of the Goddess and God.

Lughnasadh / Lammas   July 31

This festival is named after the Celtic Lugh, a god of light and fire. It celebrates the harvest of the late summer but also marks the symbolic death of the Corn King or Spirit. This spirit has to die at the end of the summer, so that life can come again next spring.

T H E

MEDIEVAL

WORLD

THE RISE OF

From the fifth century A.D., Christianity tightened its grip over Western societies and the worship of pagan gods waned. But the practice of magic continued, and, as Western culture felt threatened from outside and within, the stage was gradually set for the wholesale persecution of witches.

CHRISTIANITY

The Triumph of the Christian God

The period commonly known as the Burning Times, when many witches or suspected witches were executed, lasted from around 1450 to around 1700. For almost 1,000 years before this, however—from the emergence of Christianity as the dominant religion in the fifth century A.D. to the Burning Times—magic and witchcraft survived in Western society.

This does not mean it flourished—there were laws, executions, pronouncements, and discrimination against magic and its practitioners throughout these long centuries. But, equally, there was no systematic hounding of witches, at least not until toward the end of the period. With the benefit of hindsight, however, we can chart the gradual growth of the social and religious context within which the later witch crazes would exist.

To understand how the new Christian era moved from uneasy and sometimes hostile coexistence with magic to outright persecution, we will examine many of the stresses that have influenced society. First, let us look at how Christianity dealt with the old pagan religions and magical practices in the first years of its dominance.

Better Magicians

Though the Roman Empire itself was not to last longer than the fifth century, Christianity had by then become identified in the eyes of other societies with those civilized virtues that Rome still epitomized—virtues to which those societies still aspired. Thus the elites in many other European societies quickly adopted the faith.

It is harder to know just how quickly, and deeply, Christianity spread among the ordinary members of society. But it does seem clear that the message of Christianity appealed—in part, anyway—simply because

∧ A seventeenth-century illustration showing witches
roasting and boiling infants.

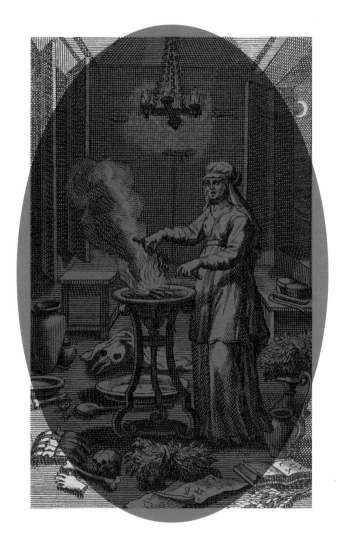

∧ A witch casts spells over a steaming cauldron—in the
early medieval world folk magic was an accepted
practice to heal the sick or tell the future.

many pagan believers could not see a huge difference between their old faiths and the new one. Like the pagan religions, Christianity had minor deities—in the form of saints—who could work miracles and heal the sick, and whose very bones could provide healing and comfort and protection from evil spirits. They were, to the ordinary believers, very good magicians whose magic was every bit as strong as, if not stronger than, that of their pagan equivalents. And the fact that the faithful would visit saints' shrines, wear amulets bearing their name, or carry bones or even dust from them all helped cement the new religion into the lives of the people. Christianity promised everything that the pagan faiths could offer and a little bit more.

Similarly, the early Christian Church showed no philosophical qualms in dealing with old pagan deities. It could, and did, cast down statues of the pagan gods and burn manuscripts. It also co-opted pagan temples and shrines for Christian worship or destroyed them altogether. The message was simple and easy to understand: The Christian God was right and powerful; all others were false.

But magic was less easy to deal with. It could exist separately from religion as well as be part of it. The folk magic used to heal the sick, tell the future, or bring good weather for crops didn't necessarily need the gods to be invoked.

Even more messy were the sensational stories of the early Christian saints and their ability to perform miracles. For how did you explain the difference between good "magic" performed by the saints, and the same magic performed by a magician? This tricky problem was tackled by St. Augustine of Hippo (354–430). In *De diversis quaestionibus* he wrote, "When magicians do the same kind of things as, on occasion, saints do, their deeds may appear similar to the naked eye, but they have a quite different intention and a quite different sanction."

The difference was this: Saints performed their magic (or miracles) for the glory of God and did so in public at the command of God; while the magicians did magic to satisfy their own ego.

This argument betrayed a philosophical weak spot in Christian thought. If it conceded that magic not only existed but could be tolerated—as long as it was done for the right reasons—then who was to decide what the right reasons were? Thus Christianity started off with an uneasy relationship with magic and magicians.

Demons and Angels

The ultimate answer for Christians in how to deal with magic, was, literally, to demonize magic and those who performed it. The concept of *daimones* or demons had already evolved in Greek thought from neutral spirits into entities that could be evil as well as benign. Now in Christian thinking they were to become wholly evil.

In a sixth-century treatise attributed (wrongly) to St. Dionysius the Areopagite, there is much detail on how the hierarchies of Heaven and Hell were organized. In Heaven the layers included Seraphim and Cherubim, down through Dominions to Archangels and Angels. Down in Hell there was a parallel, opposite grouping of devils and demons.

From this approach to angels and demons, it became quite easy to associate saints and their activities with the angels and other benign hosts of Heaven; while the demons became linked with any other magic. This reasoning meant that any witch practicing witchcraft was consorting with demons, who, in turn, were denizens of Hell.

A Pact with Satan

The Devil featured in Christianity from its very beginnings. In the New Testament, for example, Satan tries to tempt Jesus in the wilderness. The evil force is set up as a counterpart to the Son of God—and people have to make a choice of which they follow.

˄ This wood engraving (1888) depicts Jesus tempted by Satan
in the desert, as described in the Gospel of Matthew.

∧ This fifteenth-century woodcut shows a child being
   taken away from his parents by the Devil with whom
   they had made a pact.

Christianity is what could be called a partially dualist religion. It accepts that Good and Evil coexist, which makes it dualist; but it also gives Goodness clear ascendancy over Evil, which is why that dualism is only partial. This makes the Devil a problematic character. He clearly has great power, but equally clearly is not on a par with God. So how does the Devil work his evil in a God-created world, among creatures created by God—human beings?

One of the answers to this was the idea that, because humans have free will, some choose to put in their lot with the Devil. This concept of a pact with Satan was a crucial development in the early Middle Ages. If you made an agreement with Satan, then clearly you had become an enemy of God. This, of course, could not go unpunished.

Though the Devil was always present in Christian thought, his depiction was not as grotesque or as powerful in early centuries as it was to become toward the fifteenth century. Early Christian artistic images of the Devil placed more emphasis on his being a fallen angel than on the wretched, lurid form of later years. By the eleventh and twelfth centuries, however, Satan was shown in his now familiar image of horns, hooves, and tail, emphasizing his bestial, animal-like passions and lack of inhibitions. By the fifteenth century, the Devil had become a very common, very frightening, and very real image.

The Dawn of Persecution

There is a popular image that the advent of Christianity immediately led to the persecution of witches. However, this would really only begin once heresy was identified as a growing threat to the Church.

Heresy had been gnawing at the Christian Church from the beginning. There were always those—for example the Gnostics—who were essentially Christian but differed radically from the orthodox views of the Church. Yet, it was not until the eleventh century—when a group of senior figures in the Church and a number of women were executed for heresy at Orléans in France in 1022—that heretics were subjected to any formal persecution. The accused were charged with worshipping the Devil, of secret nighttime meetings, of sex orgies, of copulating with close relatives, of killing babies, and of drinking blood. None of these specific accusations were new. In former centuries Jews, pagans, and Christians had all been accused of similar acts.

What is striking here is how these grim images bear such a close resemblance to the accusations made in the later witch trials. They also borrow from Roman and Greek descriptions of mystery rites.

The heretic trials grew in momentum in the twelfth and thirteenth centuries, when the Bogomils (from Eastern Europe) and then the Cathars were ruthlessly suppressed by the Western Church. By this time the Christian Church had split East–West, with the Eastern Church's seat of power at Constantinople, while the Western (i.e. Catholic) Church was centered on Rome.

The Cathars, who were based in the South of France, believed that the Devil was associated with all things material and fleshly, and therefore all things linked to the material world were to be despised. This was going a little far for the churchmen and nobles, who rather enjoyed their trappings of power, and the Cathars were exterminated with great brutality. They were accused of all kinds of sexual practices, infanticide, and even cannibalism. Again, these accusations have a familiar ring to them. Meanwhile, the Cathars' emphasis on the Devil raised the profile of Satan in the Church's thinking.

The trials of the heretics established a blueprint that was later applied to witchcraft. Ultimately, witchcraft itself was turned into a heresy. By the late Middle Ages witches were not seen simply as practitioners of magic: They were identified with demons and therefore with the Devil. They had made a pact with the Devil and had therefore set themselves against God. This explains why witches, when found guilty, were burned in most parts of Europe—because that was what happened to heretics.

∧ The storming of Beziers, July 22, 1209, during the crusade against
Cathar heretics in southern France, initiated by Pope Innocent III.

∧ In medieval times, images emerged of witches turning
into animals and riding through the air on sticks.
Woodcut from a fifteenth century treatise on witchcraft,
De Laniis et Phitonicis Mulieribus (1489).

The Image of Witches

As far as we know, a great number of those practicing magic during the early Middle Ages were men. Certainly there is no reason from the evidence to suppose otherwise. Much of this magic was concerned with traditional concerns that existed up to the twentieth century: ensuring good crops, good weather, good health, and luck in love. These were just as much the domain of men as of women.

Yet by the fifteenth century, when the witch crazes began, witches were generally, though not exclusively, perceived as being women. Part of the reasoning for this went back to classical tradition, back to the depictions of legendary witches such as Circe and Medea by Greek and Roman writers.

Another reason was simply misogyny. Men at that time believed women to be weak, as well as superstitious and gullible. But men also felt threatened by the sexual passions of women, and believed that older women, resenting their loss of fertility as they grew older, became bitter and vengeful against men.

And by the thirteenth century a picture was beginning to emerge from folklore and chroniclers about not just who the witches were, but also the things they were supposed to do. They sucked blood, had sex with sleeping men, changed their forms into those of animals, flew through the night, and killed babies.

At the same time the legal mechanism used against both heretics and witches was tightening. By 1215 the Fourth Lateran Council had stipulated that all heretics should die if they refused to see the error of their ways. By 1233 the pace gathered still further when Pope Gregory IX empowered the Inquisition to hunt down heresy and any opponents to the Church throughout Europe. Two hundred years later Pope Eugenius IV gave the hunt fresh impetus when he told inquisitors how much he deplored the widespread practice of magic, and Satanic pacts, and urged more arrests and trials.

By now most of the religious ingredients for the impending witch crazes were in place. All those who worked with magic were in league with the Devil. Most witches were women; they were certainly all heretics. They therefore posed an internal threat to society and to God's will.

Europe Under Siege

As the West approached the fifteenth century, the peoples of Europe had been forced to face a frightening array of threats from outside. Early in the eighth century the Islamic Moors had driven hard up through Spain and threatened much of Christian Europe. They were to remain in Spain until they were finally expelled from Granada in 1492.

Elsewhere, pagan Vikings attacked much of Europe intermittently for hundreds of years, often showing great brutality along the way. Meanwhile, the Mongols ravaged large swathes of Eastern Europe from the thirteenth century, and from the fourteenth century the Muslim Turks began threatening the soft underbelly of Christian Europe, as they were to do for hundreds of years.

Add to this the grim arrival of the Black Death to European shores in the fourteenth century, killing around a third of the population, and a picture emerges of a continent under siege. It is perhaps not surprising that a society under threat looked for scapegoats. Among these were Jews and lepers, who suffered increasing persecution after the twelfth and thirteenth centuries.

Meanwhile, the Catholic Church was about to face its biggest threat yet—Protestantism. The emergence of this powerful rival to the established Church was to cause enormous conflict and dislocation throughout Europe. Each had to prove and define itself—and one of these ways would be against witchcraft.

∧ The idea that witches were in league with the Devil was perpetuated with images such as this of witches and devils dining on infants together.

THE

The late Middle Ages saw the start of widespread persecution of witches. Torture was used to extract confessions and the victims were often burned alive.

BURNING

The persecution was patchy—virulent in some areas, virtually nonexistent in others. The possible causes of this mass persecution are still debated today.

TIMES

∧ This 1626 etching by Jan van de Velde depitcts bare-breasted sorceress
  concocting her evil brew, standing within a "magic circle" scratched
  into the ground. She is surrounded by a variety of grotesque creatures.

The Rise of the Witch Craze

The widespread execution of alleged witches from the late Middle Ages until the start of the eighteenth century is easily the most controversial period in the history of witchcraft. Even the name often used by modern witches to describe this period—the Burning Times— causes disquiet among some historians. The name belies the fact that a number of witches, for example in England, North America, and Spain, were hanged and not burned at the stake. More seriously, the name implies a concerted and uniform campaign of persecution over a set period.

In fact, the execution of witches started gradually from about the fourteenth century, rose to a peak in the late sixteenth and early seventeenth centuries, and then slowly faded. Moreover, this pattern varied enormously from country to country, and even from district to district. In some areas persecution was frenetic, widespread, and seemingly out of control. In others there was barely any persecution at all.

Perhaps the most emotive question of all is just how many died during this period of two to three hundred years. The first point to make is that no one knows for sure. Trials and executions were carried out locally and not all the documentation has survived. Details were certainly not kept in central records. The best estimates range from around 40,000—which seems on the low side—to around 100,000. What can be safely stated is that claims made at the end of the nineteenth century that as many as 9 million people may have lost their lives in the witch craze do not stand up to even the smallest scrutiny.

From a historical point of view, the precise numbers of those who died is important but not the main issue. The essential task is to try to understand why many people lost their lives in a such a grotesque manner, having first been tortured into confessing to the most bizarre and unlikely of activities. For on one point there can be no doubt: this was a shameful episode in the history of Western society.

The Witch Craze Begins

There is no one starting date for the witch craze in Europe. From as early as the twelfth century there was a gradual increase in the arrest, trial, and execution of supposed heretics against orthodox Christian teaching. At the same time, it was becoming increasingly accepted among theologians and the pope-inspired inquisitions that witchcraft involved the participant making a pact with the Devil, and thus rejecting God. This made witchcraft one of the most serious heresies.

More serious still were the trials of the Knights Templar early in the fourteenth century. The Templars owned land and money, and an envious King Philip of France (Philip the Fair) saw to it that they were tried as heretics. The charges varied, and included sorcery and sodomy and the making of pacts with the Devil. This high-profile case against such a previously renowned order of knights gave credence to the idea that Satanism was real and flourishing.

The end of the fourteenth century saw a gradual increase in the number of cases of people accused of using magic combined with worshipping the Devil. In 1390, for example, two women said under torture that they had invoked the Devil as part of their magic rituals.

Continental Europe

An important development came in 1398 when the theological faculty of the University of Paris announced that the practice of harmful magic (*maleficia*) was a heresy if it entailed a pact with the Devil. Since many Christian authorities insisted that invoking any spirits during magic was itself evidence of such a pact, this pronouncement laid witchcraft wide open to charges of heresy.

∧ Jacques de Molay, the 23rd and last Grand Master of the
Knights Templar, was burned at the stake as a heretic on
March 18, 1314 on the orders of Philip IV of France.

∧ A woodcut from the *Malleus Maleficarum* (1487) shows a
witch having her neck skin flayed by four demons in the
flames of Hell, while God looks down from the Heavens.

The beginning of the fifteenth century saw a trickle of prosecutions and burnings in parts of Continental Europe. During the 1420s around 200 witches were tried around Briancon in France, close to the Italian and Swiss borders. Similar trials took place in Switzerland, at Bern, Lucerne, and Basel. Others occurred in Germany, which became, and remained, one of the centers of witch trials over the next couple of hundred years. Already the trials were beginning to show patterns. Local inquisitors would confront the accused with a list of supposed acts they had committed. These acts conformed to what were to become the standard witchcraft accusations of the times: that the witches met regularly (at Sabbats), had sex with others including the Devil, harmed or killed or even ate children, formally renounced Christ, and also mocked the sacraments of the Church. Torture was routinely used to extract these "confessions."

Another important development amid the steady trickle of witch trials came in 1484, when Pope Innocent VIII issued a "bull"—a formal written statement—that gave full papal backing for the work of local inquisitors against witchcraft.

The *Malleus Maleficarum*

The most infamous treatise against witchcraft was the *Malleus Maleficarum*, published in 1487. Its title translates into English as "the hammer of women who practice harmful magic." The *Malleus* was written by a member of the Dominican Order who was an inquisitor in south Germany, Heinrich Institoris.

The book states that key elements of witchcraft and witches included flying through the air, causing impotence in men, killing children, renouncing the Church, changing their shape into that of animals, abusing the sacraments, and, crucially, making a pact with demons or the Devil.

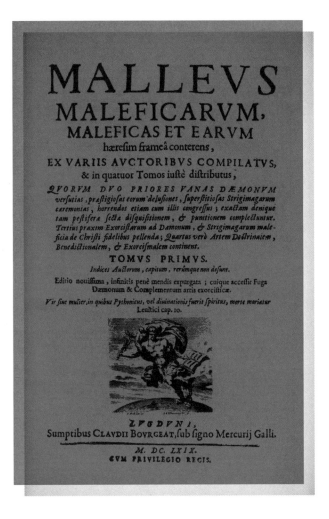

^ The *Malleus Maleficarum* (1487) was a highly influential
work and it fixed in form and image many early
superstitions concerning witchcraft.

Institoris also sets out why it is that the majority of witches, in his view, are female. Women were feeble-minded, more susceptible to superstition, morally weak, and had an insatiable sexual appetite. The author then moves to the legal process and explicitly recognizes the need for torture in obtaining the all-important confession from a witch.

It is difficult to judge how influential the *Malleus* was in inspiring later witch trials, though it was often quoted with approval by other writers on the subject. There is some evidence, for example, that it may have played a part in encouraging trials in Cologne and Trier over the next decade or so. Yet the most virulent outbreak of persecution was to occur a century after the book's original publication.

The Reformation

The early sixteenth century saw momentous religious development and most historians agree this played a part in the worst years of the witch trials. The name "Reformation" is given to the movement that caused a tremendous schism between the (Catholic) Church and reformers led by a German priest named Martin Luther. They created what was later to be called Protestantism.

The conflicts and wars between these two faiths over the next century and a half caused massive chaos throughout European society. The Catholic Church had fought successfully against heretics, but here was a popular movement that soon established itself as a serious rival. Meanwhile, Protestants believed the Catholic Church had warped some of the early teachings of Christianity. But both sides agreed on one thing: witchcraft was evil and a sign of the Devil's work. Luther himself declared in 1522 that witches were the "Devil's whores"—a phrase that left little room for doubt as to where he stood on the issue.

So there was no respite from witch trials from either side of the religious divide. In fact, by the second half of the century, trials were on the increase, notably in Germany. In what is now Austria the Catholic ruler Rudolf II presided over widespread persecutions. France, too, was the center for a number of large trials.

Early in the seventeenth century the trials reached a grisly peak, especially in Germany, where the Catholic–Protestant tension ignited the Thirty Years War (1618–48). Cologne saw a spate of trials at this time, spurred on by Archbishop Frederick of Bavaria, as did Bamberg, where the ultra-zealous Prince-Bishop Johann Georg II oversaw the burning of some 600 witches or more in the space of only a decade. The trials flourished in both Catholic and Protestant areas of Germany. Large-scale witch hunts also began in the first decade of the century in the Basque region of France.

Meanwhile the craze spread northward in Europe to Scandinavia, which had remained relatively immune to the hunts of the sixteenth century. The worst period for trials in Jutland in Denmark was between 1617 and 1625. In Sweden and Finland (then part of Sweden) the majority of witch trials came much later still, in the 1660s and 1670s. The Swedish trials, in particular, were marked by the apparent evidence that hundreds of children had been victims of, or witnesses to, the witches' Sabbats.

The Spanish Inquisition

The picture across Europe was far from uniform, however. In Spain, for example, where the supposedly brutal Spanish Inquisition operated, relatively few witches or alleged witches were burned. As early as 1526 the main council of the organization, the Suprema, pointed out to its officials that misfortunes such as crop failure should be blamed on God's wrath or even simply bad weather—not on witches.

More importantly still, the Suprema carried out an inquiry in 1612 into the recent (and very rare) burning of five witches—out of 29 accused—in the Navarre region. The author of the inquiry report, a lawyer named

^ A woodcut from 1520 shows the hanging of a farm woman
who had been declared by the Spanish Inquisition to be
possessed by demons.

∧ A seventeenth-century French print that depicts themes
   of occultism, poisoning, and other crimes thought to be
   perpetrated by women.

Alonso de Salazar Frias, concluded in it that there was "not the slightest evidence that a single act of witchcraft has really occurred." Salazar added that in his view at least three-quarters of the defendants had wrongly confessed both to their crimes and to the involvement of others.

Thereafter, the Spanish Inquisition continued to draw a strong distinction between heresy/Devil worship on one hand and witchcraft and sorcery on the other; the latter not warranting automatic execution. However, this did not stop some civil authorities, for example in Catalonia, hanging a number of witches in the 1620s, often at the insistence of the local populations.

This complex situation in Spain reflects that fact that even at the height of the witch craze there were dissenting voices against the trials.

Nicholas Rémy

A string of virulent publications appeared in the late sixteenth and early seventeenth centuries, each supporting the persecution of witches and urging the authorities to be ever more rigorous. One of the most important of these was a work called *Demonolatry*, published in 1595 and written by a French lawyer, Nicholas Rémy (1530–1616). Rémy was one of the most determined witch hunters of his time. Coming from a wealthy family of lawyers, Rémy is thought to have witnessed witch trials as a boy. Certainly his own determination to root out and execute witches seems to have had personal roots. Within a few days of Rémy refusing to give money to an elderly woman beggar, his eldest son died. For some reason—perhaps through his experience of witch trials from childhood—the lawyer blamed the boy's death on witchcraft. Rémy personally had the woman prosecuted and she was convicted of bewitching his son. This was the start of more than ten years of witch hunting by Rémy.

In his book the lawyer claimed to know of 900 cases where witches had been convicted and executed in the Lorraine area of France in the previous 15 years. He wrote lurid descriptions of the supposed activities of the devil-worshipping witches, their sex orgies, drinking, feasting, their pacts with the Devil, and their ability to poison people. This detail, supported as it was by apparent real-life evidence from real court cases, made the book a big success, and it supplanted the *Malleus* as the book of choice for witch persecutors. Like the *Malleus*, *Demonolatry* also drew on descriptions from the classical writers from Homer onward to consolidate the case against witches and Devil worship.

Urged on by Rémy and others, the largest number of witch trials and burnings across Europe came in the period from about 1580 to about 1650. They dwindled after this time, though a trickle of cases continued into the eighteenth century. The last reported execution of a witch in Austria was in 1756; in 1722 in Denmark; in France in 1745; Bavaria in Germany in 1775; and 1782 in Switzerland. By these dates, though, the witch craze had emphatically died out.

The British Isles

In England the link between witchcraft (or sorcery) and heresy was not made. So, while successive English administrations—both Protestant and Catholic—cheerfully burned heretics during the sixteenth century, they did not burn witches.

The main legislation in sixteenth-century England was that passed under Queen Elizabeth I in 1563. This provided punishment for a variety of acts of witchcraft, though offenses were to be tried by the civil courts and not linked to heresy. The use of magic to harm others did not lead to automatic execution; however, anyone found guilty of killing someone by sorcery did suffer the death penalty—as any other murderer would. A number of alleged witches were tried and hanged under this legislation, notably in Essex.

∧ A woodcut featured in *The History of Witches and Wizards* (1720) shows the "sink or float" method of seeking out witches.

^ A woodcut by Hans Baldung entitled *The Witches* (1510) reinforces the image of witches as grotesque and malevolent.

The reaction in England toward witchcraft altered in the seventeenth century. This was largely due to the accession of a new monarch in 1603, James I, who was also James VI of Scotland. In Scotland, James had been convinced of the menace of witchcraft after a series of trials from 1590 in which some 300 people were charged with witchcraft. Some of the accusations included alleged plots to raise storms to attack James as he sailed to and from Denmark to collect his bride, Anne.

Soon after James became King of England, Parliament quickly passed new laws against witchcraft, which provided for an automatic death penalty for anyone causing harm to people or property by witchcraft. This 1604 law, however, still did not link witchcraft specifically with Devil worship or heresy.

The king's newly authorized version of the Bible also translated references to people who practiced bad magic or who poisoned others as "witch." This misleading translation, which may have been done as a deliberate act of propaganda, has had an enormous impact over the centuries. For example, some Christians still cite the passage at Exodus 22:18, which in the King James Bible reads, "Thou shalt not suffer a witch to live." The original Hebrew word translated as "witch" actually means "a woman who performs evil/harmful magic."

The new legislation in England saw a rise in the number of witch trials, though by 1616 James himself was becoming concerned that innocent people were being convicted on flimsy evidence; and he personally intervened in at least one case, in Leicester.

The Witch-Finder General

The witch trials in England were still erratic and spasmodic until the start of the Civil War in the 1640s, which caused widespread turmoil in the country as Royalists fought with Parliamentarians for supremacy. Into this chaotic period strode a Puritan and failed lawyer, Matthew

Hopkins. In a brief period from 1644 to 1646, Hopkins was responsible for the execution of at least 230 witches—probably more than half the total put to death in England during the length of the entire witch hunts.

The self-styled Witch-Finder General employed the notorious "swimming" or "dunking" technique of assessing whether someone was a witch. Those accused were thrown into the water and, if the water (which was part of nature and thus God's creation) rejected them and they floated, they were guilty. If they sank, they were innocent—though of course they could drown.

Hopkins's reign of mass witch trials ended quickly. His many critics complained of his exorbitant fees, his brutality, and the fact that clearly innocent people were being accused. His death in 1647 did not mean the end of all witch trials in England, but they were certainly not prosecuted with the same zeal. The last execution of a witch in Scotland was in 1727. In England, Jane Clarke and her children were tried but acquitted in 1717; and by 1736 the harsh penalties of the 1604 laws were repealed.

The Victims

Women bore the brunt of the witch hunts. The exact figures are unknown, but estimates suggest that around 75 percent of those executed were female.

One reason why so many more woman were accused was that, quite simply, women were regarded as being more likely to be capable of being in league with the Devil. Satan was regarded as a masculine character, and lust as part of his personality. It followed, then, that women were his natural sexual partners. The *Malleus* makes it clear that women were often regarded as having what it called insatiable sexual appetites.

∧ This vivid image shows witches being burned alive in
Dernburg, Germany, in 1555.

∧ Appalling torture methods were inflicted on those
accused of witchcraft in order to extract confessions.

Trial, Torture, and Ordeal

Witches could be accused on the basis of what was called *indicia*—inferences. Someone's child might have died just after it came into contact with the defendant. Or a person might have fallen ill after an argument with the accused. These were enough to bring the initial charges. But, as even the *Malleus* accepted, this "evidence" alone was not enough—what was needed was the accused to confess. This was why the use of torture was so widespread.

The tortures used were horrific. Thumbscrews, red-hot irons, setting people alight, beatings, and immersing hands or feet in boiling oil were just some of them. If victims didn't confess under torture it didn't mean they were innocent: it meant, simply, that the Devil was helping them.

As well as the swimming and dunking test, another extrajudicial and grotesque means of detecting a witch was the use of a process called "pricking." Each witch was supposed to have a "Devil's mark," which was a sign of initiation from Satan as part of his pact with the witch. It was believed that this mark, which of course could be hidden anywhere on the body, was insensitive to pain. So the accused might be stripped, shaven all over, then "pricked" with a sharp instrument until a patch was found that did not appear to hurt.

Causes of the Witch Hunts

The debate about what caused the witch hunts is likely to continue as more detailed studies are carried out into local outbreaks of persecution. There are already, though, a large number of theories.

An argument used by some feminists is that the witch hunts were a classic and extreme example of a patriarchal society brutally repressing women. Society was undeniably misogynistic in the fifteenth, sixteenth, and seventeenth centuries, when the witch hunts were at their most virulent. But, then, society was equally so before and after the witch hunts. The theory also does not take into account the fact that some 25 percent of victims were men—and in some areas a majority were. Nor does it account for the differing focal points of the hunts. In some areas there were barely any witch trials at all. What can be said is that ongoing misogyny, the identification of women with witchcraft, and a latent fear of women's sexuality formed an important background to the witch crazes.

Another factor often given as a cause is the Catholic–Protestant conflict that scarred much of Europe during this period. It is true that an area such as Germany (at the time a collection of states of various sizes), which was most affected by the Reformation and Counter-Reformation, also saw some of the worst persecution of witches. Meanwhile, the worst period for witch trials in England came during the Civil War, a conflict that had a religious backdrop as well as a political cause. What was certainly true was that both religious traditions, faced with rivals, felt the need to be assertive of their beliefs and to define where their faith started and ended. The attacks on witchcraft could be seen as part of this process.

Yet the witch crazes began, albeit gradually, before the Reformation. And by no means were all the witch hunts in areas suffering religious turmoil. Religious conflict of the time may well have been a contributory factor, but cannot be seen as the sole cause of the witch hunts.

Society's view of magic is also an important factor. This period saw a rise of interest in what might be described as natural magic. This Neoplatonist approach believed that high magic was morally neutral and was concerned with understanding the nature of God's world. As such, it was linked with chemistry, physics, and alchemy. Its exponents included John Dee (1527–1608), who was a court astrologer to Queen Elizabeth I of England. One of the most learned men of his time, Dee had a lifelong interest in so-called "high" magic, or natural magic, and devoted himself to the pursuit of mystical and magical knowledge.

∧ John Dee (1527–1608) was an English astrologer, alchemist, and mathematician at the court of Queen Elizabeth I, and had a deep interest in magical knowledge.

∧   In this etching based on *Witch's Initiation* (1640s) by David Teniers
    the Younger, an older woman is teaching magic to her daughter,
    while on the right a young naked woman is seen surrounded by
    old witches and demons, preparing to ascend the chimney.

The opposing Aristotelian view, as expressed by the thirteenth-century theologian Thomas Aquinas, was that all magic involved the use of spirits—who were demons.

The heated debate between these two sides brought the whole subject of magic and its morality to the attention of the European elite—the very kind of people who wrote treatises, preached sermons, made laws, and prosecuted criminals.

There is evidence that the witch hunts were at their fiercest when a strong local person of influence, religious or political, was personally motivated to pursue witches—for example, Matthew Hopkins in England or Johann Georg II in Bamberg. Some outbreaks appeared to be linked to local food shortages, bad harvests, or disease. Another claim is that the witch hunts flourished where there was weak government, or where officials felt obliged to follow the whims of local communities.

One important way of looking at the witch hunts is to consider their psychological meaning. People suffering misfortune often blame others for their bad luck. The easiest people to blame are those on the margins—the outsiders, people who are different. This happened to Jews and lepers in the Middle Ages. The same may well have happened to those thought to be connected with witchcraft. Once a few people have been accused, the accusations can take on a life of their own, and paranoia can sweep through a community. Then the usual rules of society are thrown away.

So the search for one clear cause of the witch crazes is likely to prove elusive. The conditions of social unrest, aggressive theology, and uncertainty about the practice of magic, mixed with local conditions and a natural human desire to blame others all seem to have played their part in this tragic episode in history.

< A woman is tied on a
  pedestal to be burned
  as a witch, in the middle
  of a large crowd.

WITCHES' TOOLS

The keeping of ritual tools is important for witches, whether they are part of a coven or work alone. The aim of both ritual and tools is to focus the person's will on the object of the magic being performed.

Here are some of the main tools used by witches:

ALTAR

This is used to place the other ritual tools upon and is always itself placed inside the magic circle—usually facing toward the north, though others place it to the east.

ATHAME

Traditionally a black-handled knife, it is not used for cutting physical objects but for focusing an individual's will and, by waving its point, for "drawing" ritual shapes such as pentagrams and circles.

BELL

Sometimes used to announce the start of a ritual or the casting of a magic circle. It can also be hung up as a protective object.

BESOM/BROOM

In late medieval times the witch became associated with the

broom, possibly because riding a broom over fields had been performed in pagan fertility rites. Brooms are now sometimes used to symbolically "clean" areas of negative energy.

BOOK OF SHADOWS

Before the revival of modern Witchcraft these were known as grimoires. They are the books of spells and magical rituals performed by a particular tradition or coven of witchcraft.

CANDLES

Used in various colors, candles are an essential element for much magical work, representing fire and creating the right atmosphere.

CAULDRON

Long associated with witches, cauldrons represent transformation and change, and symbolize the womb. Often used for the burning of a small fire in rituals.

CHALICE

Holds water or wine used in rituals. The chalice represents fertility and receptivity. Like the cauldron, it also symbolizes the womb—while the wand is a phallic symbol.

CORD

The tying and untying of knots assists in releasing energy for spells.

ROBE

Some witches perform rituals naked or "sky-clad"; however many prefer to use a special robe for performing magic. Normally witches are barefoot during ceremonies.

WAND

Made from wood, the wand can be used instead of an athame. The preferred wood is hazel, though willow and birch are often used as well. A wand may be used to invoke the Goddess and God.

NEW

WORLD,

OLD

*The New World was a new
beginning for many Europeans,
but was not immune from the
witch crazes. Some Puritans
preached that New England was
under attack from witchcraft
as a punishment from God.
The horrors of Salem in 1692,
however, effectively ended the
hunting of witches.*

HORRORS

MEMORABLE PROVIDENCES,

Relating to

WITCHCRAFTS

And POSSESSIONS.

A Faithful Account of many Wonderful and Surprising Things, that have befallen several Bewitched and Poſſeſſed Perſons in New-England.
Particularly, A NARRATIVE of the marvellous Trouble and Releef Experienced by a pious Family in Boſton, very lately ,and ſadly moleſted with EVIL SPIRITS.
Whereunto is added,
A Diſcourſe delivered unto a Congregation in Boſton, on the Occaſion of that Illuſtrious Providence. As alſo
A Diſcourſe delivered unto the ſame Congregation; on the occaſion of an horrible Self-Murder Committed in the Town.
With an Appendix, in vindication of a Chapter in a late Book of Remarkable Providences, from the Calumnies of a Quaker at Pen.ſilvania.

Written By Cotton Mather, Miniſter of the Goſpel.

And Recommended by the Miniſters of Boſton and Charleſton

Printed at Boſton in N. England by R. P. 1689.
Sold by Joſeph Brunning, at his Shop at the Corner of the Priſon-Lane next the Exchange.

∧ *Memorable Providences Relating to Witchcrafts and Possessions* was written by Cotton Mather, a Puritan minister from Boston in 1689, who strongly believed in the dangers of witchcraft.

Witches in New England

In their approach to witchcraft, the settlements in the New World tended to reflect the practices of their mother countries. The inquisitions in the Spanish-American colonies were as alert as their counterpart in Spain to heresy and could be ruthless in their treatment. But, also like their counterpart in Spain, these inquisitions saw a distinction between, on the one hand, simple magic or sorcery and, on the other, a determined departure from standard Catholic beliefs.

The settlers in New England tended to follow the English approach to witchcraft. The modern view of witchcraft in North America is of course dominated by the dramatic events at Salem in 1692 (see pages 148–69). Yet the horrors of that small Massachusetts settlement were highly unusual both in scale and frenzy in the English-speaking world. At all other times, events in New England closely mirrored the relatively low level of prosecutions and the relative absence of hysteria seen in England. The settlers were in fact governed by the English legislation passed in 1604 soon after the accession of James I, which did not explicitly link witchcraft to Devil worship and heresy but put more emphasis on witches causing harm by magic. Those executed in New England were hanged, never burned at the stake.

However, the idea that witches could make a pact with the Devil did feature in North American accusations of witchcraft. The writings of Europeans on the subject of witchcraft and demons were well known among the educated in New England, and they would have been familiar with the witch furor that had been raging on the other side of the Atlantic.

One such work was by William Perkins, an English Puritan whose *Discourse on the Damned Art of Witchcraft*, published in 1608, became a standard text on the topic in the English-speaking world. According to Perkins, good indications that someone was a witch included their having a quarrel with someone, followed by an act of misfortune; a curse, followed by someone's death; or the opinion of "men of honesty and credit" that a person was a witch. Such circumstantial events were often the basis for accusations in New England, though alone they were not sufficient for a conviction.

The first executions of witches in New England occurred in the late 1640s, just after a rash of witch trials in the southeast of England inspired by the self-appointed Witch-Finder General, Matthew Hopkins (see pages 123–4). The first recorded New England victim was Alice Young, a woman from Windsor, Connecticut, who was tried and hanged as a witch in 1647; other than that, very little is recorded of the case.

The Hartford Witch Hunt

The biggest New England witch hunt of the middle part of the seventeenth century took place at Hartford, Connecticut. In all, at least eight people were accused of witchcraft and three people were executed: a woman called Mary Barnes, and a husband and wife named Nathaniel and Rebecca Greensmith. In North America as in Europe, the victims of witch trials were largely women, but this did not mean some men were not accused and executed as well. Typically, the men who were accused were related in some way to women who had already been accused of witchcraft. In this case, Rebecca Greensmith was accused of witchcraft and she then made a statement that incriminated her husband.

The case came after a local woman, Ann Cole, began suffering fits of what were diagnosed as "diabolical possession" in 1662. One of those she accused of causing her affliction was Rebecca Greensmith. Curiously, Rebecca seems to have confessed to "familiarity with the Devil" and described meetings she held in woods with other local women.

These kinds of confessions, in which the accused not only admitted their own guilt but accused others as well, often had a "snowball" effect and sometimes led to the mass accusations and panic that constituted a witch craze.

^ The frontispiece of Matthew Hopkins' book *The Discovery of Witches* (1647).

∧ Cotton Mather (1663–1728) was an official observer at the
infamous Salem witch trials.

However, after the Hartford cases there were no executions for witchcraft in New England for 25 years—and even then it was an isolated case in Boston. This hardly suggests a society that was on the verge of panic about Satan and his followers.

In many cases, even where juries were happy to convict, judges could intervene to stop the case leading to execution. This occurred in the case of Katherine Harrison, a wealthy widow from Wethersfield, Connecticut. In 1668 she was accused of witchcraft and ultimately faced two juries. The first could not agree on a verdict; the second found her guilty. However, according to legal documents of the time, magistrates later ruled that they "cannot concur with [the jury] so as to sentence her to death" and she was released—though she was told to leave the colony.

Increase and Cotton Mather

The story of witchcraft in New England in the seventeenth century is closely bound up with the lives of two men: Increase Mather and his son Cotton. Both were to influence the mood of society in the build-up to events at Salem, and both had important roles in its aftermath.

Increase Mather was a Puritan minister who held strong views on obedience to the Bible and all its teachings. A very influential person in the political arena, he helped to negotiate a new charter for the colony after the Glorious Revolution in England in 1688.

Increase believed that the growing number of problems in New England, including disease, attacks from Indians, and the presence of witchcraft, were signs that God was displeased and that society needed to rediscover its moral purpose.

His book *An Essay for the Recording of Illustrious Providence*, published in 1684, proved immensely popular. It set out Increase's vision of Puritans fighting on God's side against the Devil and his hordes for control of the New World. It also contained some fairly excitable descriptions of witchcraft and supernatural events. Although Increase may have stoked apprehension about witches, he did later express concern about the types of evidence used in some trials to convict alleged witches. In 1693 he published a book called *Cases of Conscience*, which outlined some of his concerns.

Like his father, Cotton Mather took a keen interest in witchcraft and all things supernatural. Cotton was also a Puritan minister in Boston, and in that city was involved in the case of Mary Glover, who in 1688 became the first person hanged for witchcraft in New England for 25 years. Cotton drew on this and other experiences for his influential 1689 book *Memorable Providences Relating to Witchcrafts and Possessions*.

This book, which some consider an important backdrop to the hysteria witnessed just three years later at Salem, showed in particular Cotton's belief in the reality and danger of witchcraft and the Devil. He painted a siege-like picture of the Puritans living in a land that had once been the "Devil's Territories," and he accepted all the evidence and descriptions that he had heard from witchcraft trials across Europe; he also believed all the current thinking on witchcraft expressed by writers such as William Perkins.

After the evident travesty of justice at Salem, at which he had been an official observer, Cotton Mather did express some doubts about the use of "spectral evidence"—whereby a witness claimed to see the spirit of the accused even though the person was in another place at the time—to convict people. He was later to play down the role he had performed in the events of Salem. But in 1693 he become involved in the case of a Boston woman named Margaret Rule, who Cotton Mather believed was possessed by "evil angels," at the instigation of one of her neighbors.

Salem was undoubtedly a turning point in the treatment of witchcraft in North America and its very ferocity helped ensure that such events could not easily happen again.

The Wonders of the Invisible World :

Being an Account of the

TRYALS

OF

Several Witches,

Lately Excuted in

NEW-ENGLAND:

And of several remarkable Curiosities therein Occurring.

Together with,

I. Observations upon the Nature, the Number, and the Operations of the Devils.

II. A short Narrative of a late outrage committed by a knot of Witches in Swede-Land, very much resembling, and so far explaining, that under which New-England has laboured.

III. Some Councels directing a due Improvement of the Terrible things lately done by the unusual and amazing Range of Evil-Spirits in New-England.

IV. A brief Discourse upon those Temptations which are the more ordinary Devices of Satan.

By COTTON MATHER.

Published by the Special Command of his EXCELLENCY the Goveneur of the Province of the Massachusetts-Bay in New-England.

Printed first, at Boston in New-England ; and Reprinted at London, for John Dunton, at the Raven in the Poultry. 1693.

∧ Cotton Mather's 1693 book *The Wonders of the Invisible World* dealt with witchcraft delusions in New England and defended his role in the events at Salem.

∧ A nineteenth-century depiction of the Salem witch trials by artist Joseph E. Baker.

SALEM :

The events at Salem, Massachusetts, have gone down in history as a symbol for mass panic and intolerance within a society.

A TOWN

This infamous witch hunt was by far the worst in North America and by far the best documented. Yet historians still argue about what caused it.

POSSESSED

∧ The home of Philip and Mary English, prominent members of society in Salem; they too were accused of witchcraft and fled to New York to avoid prosecution. Illustration from *A Book of New England Legends and Folk Lore in Prose and Poetry* (1884).

The Grip of Fear

In early 1692, the unexplained illness of two young girls in a small town on the east coast of America triggered the events that were to have a profound impact on the story of witchcraft in North America and elsewhere.

The two girls—Elizabeth Parris and Abigail Williams—lived in Salem, Massachusetts, and the accusations they later made led to the arrest of 141 people for practicing witchcraft, and to the execution of twenty of them: nineteen were hanged after conviction; the twentieth was crushed beneath heavy stones for refusing even to stand trial. Salem had indeed become a place possessed—possessed by fear, anger, hatred, and ignorance.

The events in Salem in the late seventeenth century are now synonymous with intolerance and collective fear; Arthur Miller's famous play *The Crucible* (1953) dramatized the chilling events of Salem's witch hunt to powerful effect. Miller was not the first or last to see a clear link between the mood pervading Salem and the fevered hunt for suspected communists in the United States led by Senator Joseph McCarthy during the 1950s.

But there is also another lasting significance to the Salem trials. Though the executions at Salem were to be the last for witchcraft in America, they have had a large influence on the way people perceive witches. The underlying assumption of the Salem trials was that to be a witch was to be in league with the Devil and thus anti-Christian. And so uniquely powerful and ingrained is the image of Salem to this day that it is an assumption that many who practice witchcraft today are still trying to alter.

Seventeenth-century Salem

The events of Salem remain by far the most striking example of how the very fear and suspicion of witchcraft could have a corrosive effect on society and its behavior. At that time, the Devil was considered a very real and present enemy, whose allies lived among society, trying to destroy God's will. In isolated outposts such as Salem the fear could be very real. These terrors had in part been inspired by such eminent Puritan ministers as Cotton Mather (see pages 143–4), whose 1689 book *Memorable Providences Relating to Witchcrafts and Possessions* spoke powerfully of the demonic threat to New England from the forces of Evil.

There were practical reasons, too, why the people of Salem felt that God was perhaps angry with them: The constant threat of attack from American Indians was very strong. Smallpox was a perennial danger, and the winter of 1691–2 was severe. There were also feuds among the elite families within Salem Village and between the village and Salem Town. Together they were a potent combination into which the events of January 1692 were to explode.

Fortune-telling

Betty Parris and her cousin Abigail Williams were living with Betty's father, the local preacher the Reverend Samuel Parris. During the long, dreary winter the young pair—Betty was nine, Abigail two years older—had played divination games with friends. The family's female slave Tituba, an Arawak Indian bought by the family in Barbados, may also have been present. This circle met regularly, swapping stories, and indulging in fortune-telling. This involved the then common practice of cracking an egg into a glass and interpreting what they saw.

It is perhaps not too difficult now to imagine how this set of circumstances could cause some psychological reaction in excitable young people. The nights were dark and cold, and as we have seen there was fear of attack, poverty, and disease in a settlement already hit by division. Moreover, in one of the fortune-telling eggs the girls are said to have seen the specter of a coffin, an image powerful enough to upset any

∧ Barbadian slave Tituba was one of the first women
accused of witchcraft during the Salem witch trials;
she was imprisoned but later released.

∧ Record of the slave Tituba's testimony at the Salem
witchcraft trials in 1692.

SALEM: A TOWN POSSESSED

impressionable young person.

Whatever the immediate cause, by January 20, Betty and Abigail were in a disturbed state and suffering violent fits, trancelike states, and bouts of screaming. Childish curiosity had turned to something like panic.

The local doctor, William Griggs, was called in to treat the girls but was puzzled by their condition. Soon the "affliction," as it came to be called, had spread to five other girls, Ann Putnam, Elizabeth Hubbard, Mary Walcott, Mary Warren, and Mercy Lewis. The medical man declared himself beaten by the outbreak and sought to blame it on factors beyond his control. The Devil, he said, was upon the girls.

This bold assertion by Dr. Griggs had unforeseen consequences. Mary Sibley, an aunt of one of the girls, thought she had the answer to who was behind such Satanic attacks. She persuaded Tituba and her husband John to bake what was known as a "witch cake." This was made from ordinary rye meal and the urine of the "afflicted" girls, and was supposed to be able to help the girls reveal the identity of any witches who had bewitched them.

The unfortunate creature who ate the cake was the Parris family dog, and from the dog's reaction the "countercharm" of the cake was thought to be working. The girls, now apparently able to reveal their tormentors, pointed the finger at Tituba and two other women, Sarah Good and Sarah Osborne.

All three women were in a weak position in the eyes of seventeenth-century society—Tituba was a slave, Sarah Good a habitually homeless woman who had begged for food, and Sarah Osborne an elderly woman who hadn't been to church for a year.

The three women were arrested on February 29, 1692, and examined by two magistrates. During the questioning, the afflicted girls would scream and tumble around on the floor of the room, but despite this intimidating atmosphere Sarah Good and Sarah Osborne steadfastly denied the accusations. Tituba, however, confessed to meeting the Devil, describing at one point meeting a tall man from Boston (interpreted as Satan by her questioners) and being forced to sign a book that had other names in it.

The witch hunt was now building an unstoppable momentum. Over the next three months more and more people were implicated in the supposed evil conspiracy, mostly women, including hitherto pillars of the local church community. By the end of May the mood in Salem was at fever pitch, and the newly appointed governor of Massachusetts, Sir William Phips, who had just arrived at the colony, felt obliged to establish a special court of "oyer and terminer" to try the backlog of cases (the term comes from the medieval Anglo-French, *oyer et terminer*, meaning "to hear and to determine" and refers to courts which had the power to try serious criminal cases).

The Trials

The first person to be tried was Bridget Bishop, already a controversial character in Salem and a shrewd choice by the prosecution to be the first on the stand. She had been married three times, ran two taverns, dressed flamboyantly, and had been accused of witchcraft 12 years before.

There had also reportedly been dolls or "poppets"—with pins stuck in them—found in the wall of a house where Bishop had once lived. Such a background, coupled with the accusations of the "afflicted"—who eventually numbered more than 40—was enough to convict Bishop in the eyes of the jury. She was hanged at Gallows Hill on June 10, 1692.

This first trial had been based on the evidence of Bishop's reputation and past behavior, evidence that the modern person would consider at best merely circumstantial and grossly inadequate. Later trials lacked even this, and used what was called "spectral evidence." This was the claim by "afflicted" persons that they had seen the accused's spirit or "spectral form" appear to them even while the accused's physical body was elsewhere. It was naturally hard to refute such evidence.

^ A nineteenth-century wood engraving of the hanging
of two "witches" at Salem in 1692.

∧ A nineteenth-century illustration of the Reverend George Burroughs being accused of witchcraft during the Salem witch trials.

Though one of the judges, Nathaniel Saltonstall, stepped down from the court after the first trial—probably in protest at the acceptance of spectral evidence—the tone was set for the rest of the long, hot summer as the trials continued.

Testimonies

Many of the testimonies at Salem highlight what now seem desperately unfair trials. The most striking of these was the case of Rebecca Nurse, a woman in her seventies, pious and generally respected by the community. Though accused by one of the afflicted girls of being a witch, Nurse was originally cleared at her trial at the end of June. By then more than 30 local people had signed a petition saying they had seen no evidence of witchcraft from her.

But when the jury acquitted Nurse, some of the afflicted girls in the courtroom fell about in fits and faints. The judges then suggested to the jury that they might want to reconsider their verdict and this time Nurse was convicted. Despite a statement from a juror and a plea to the governor, Nurse was eventually hanged on July 19.

Another execution that caused particular disquiet in Salem was that of George Burroughs. Burroughs had briefly been the minister at Salem some years before and was by all accounts a colorful character. Just before his execution, Burroughs recited the Lord's Prayer flawlessly, something that no witch was supposed to be able to do. This caused a stir among the crowd, who began to suggest that the minister be reprieved. However, Cotton Mather was at the execution and in a powerful speech quickly persuaded the doubting crowd that Burroughs had been found guilty by the court and thus deserved to die.

The Case of John Proctor

Proctor was the first man to be accused of witchcraft in the Salem trials and was a victim of his own outspoken doubts about the presence of witchcraft. A large, bad-tempered man, Proctor threatened his servant Mary Warren after she started having fits like the other afflicted, and his harsh approach seems to have brought her back to her senses— temporarily. However, the fact that Proctor was so public in his skepticism about the presence of witchcraft helped seal his fate. Before his trial Proctor alleged that torture had been used to gain some confessions of witchcraft, and he appealed to clergy in Boston who were known to be sympathetic. Nonetheless, he was tried, convicted on "spectral evidence" of charges that he practiced witchcraft, and executed; though his wife Elizabeth escaped hanging because she was pregnant at the time.

Giles Corey, a farmer, aged eighties, and a regular churchgoer, was accused of witchcraft but refused even to stand trial. His punishment for this contempt of court was to be pressed to death by large stones. It took two full days to kill Corey in this way. Exactly why Corey chose not to stand trial is a mystery. The most likely explanation is that this strong-willed man knew that death was almost certain after his trial, and he wanted to show his contempt for the whole process.

The Fear Subsides

As the autumn of 1692 wore on, the people of Salem and surrounding areas grew more and more uneasy at the witch trials. The examples of Rebecca Nurse and Giles Corey were fresh in people's minds. Doubts were raised about allowing the so-called "spectral evidence" against the accused. Increase Mather, a man of considerable influence, added to the debate by attacking the reliance on spectral evidence. In his book *Cases of Conscience* he later declared that it was better that

∧ Late-nineteenth century engraving of the execution of former Salem minister George Burroughs, which caused much disquiet.

∧ Bridget Bishop was the first woman in Salem to be
tried for practicing witchcraft. She was convicted
and hanged in June 1692.

"ten suspected witches should escape than that one innocent person should be condemned."

Under this growing pressure, the governor, Sir William Phips, finally forbade the court to allow this type of evidence, and at the end of October dissolved the special court of oyer and terminer altogether. Later trials produced a string of acquittals—and in May 1693 Phips pardoned all the remaining accused. By then, however, 19 people had been hanged for witchcraft, one man crushed to death for refusing to stand trial, and at least four others had died in prison awaiting trial. Years later Ann Putnam, one of the chief accusers among the afflicted, issued a public apology in which she stated she had meant no ill will to anyone and had been "deluded by Satan" into making the false accusations.

What Caused the Witch Hunt at Salem?

The people of seventeenth-century Salem were not the only ones who believed in the physical presence of the Devil or who felt under pressure as a community. So why did such a virulent witch hunt happen only there and not elsewhere in New England? The causes are still debated. Some have blamed a power struggle within the community, with the Reverend Parris and his young family being used as pawns to attack rival factions. Another theory is that the clinical hysteria demonstrated in Salem was the product of the repressed Puritan mind, and that the witch hunt was the outward expression of inner sexual and spiritual turmoil.

At least one modern historian has suggested that some of the accused—notably Bridget Bishop—were practicing witchcraft. A common theory was that the girls simply made all the stories up out of spite, and events spiraled out of control, forcing them to go along with it.

The truth is likely to lie in a combination of factors. The young girls whose affliction started the witch hunt took part in fortune-telling. In the dark depths of winter, this harmless pastime does appear somehow to have set off a chain reaction of fear. The clinical hysteria that they showed defeated the examinations of local doctors, and it was common medical practice of the time to blame insoluble conditions on the supernatural.

At the same time, the seventeenth-century mindset was ready and able to believe in the intervention of the Devil and his agents, and in Salem there was more reason than in most places to look for explanations for a time of hardship. Once people starting confessing to witchcraft, the hunt quickly gained momentum.

None of these factors alone explain why Salem suffered such an extreme outbreak of paranoia, but together they add up to a combustible cocktail of causes.

Lasting Legacy

The trials at Salem continue to hold a grip on the public imagination more than 300 years later—in part because they tell us how humans behave when fear and ignorance replace reason; in part for the practical reason that the trials are the best documented in the English-speaking world.

People in seventeenth-century America believed witchcraft existed, and at certain levels it was even tolerated in society. But once a community felt under threat this uneasy tolerance was blown away and witchcraft became a convenient scapegoat for that society's problems.

^ An elderly woman with her hands held out in a gesture of innocence is led away during the Salem witch trials.

CONCLUSION

Why the Witch Hunts Ended

Just as there was no precise date for the start of the Burning Times or witch craze, so there was no precise time at which they ended.

The cases of trials to execute witches as heretics dwindled in the eighteenth century. The last executions for witchcraft in France were in 1745, in Denmark it was in 1722 and in Austria 1756. The extreme case of Salem effectively brought the witch hunts to an end in North America. By 1736 the 1604 law on witchcraft governing both England and North America had been replaced with new, less repressive legislation.

The reasons for this decline are as complex as the factors that caused them. Many of the circumstances that are often regarded as helping to cause the hunts—wars, population upheaval, famines, religious conflicts—continued into the eighteenth century. The world did not suddenly become a place of tolerance, democracy, and shiny liberalism.

What seems to have happened, though, is that the doubts about the fairness of the witch trials—doubts that had existed almost from their beginning—began to grow stronger. The extraordinary way in which witch trials were conducted, the type of evidence that was allowed, and the indiscriminate use of torture are not just aberrations judged by modern standards. They were aberrations by the standards of the times. The legal framework was already in place in the sixteenth and seventeenth centuries, which could and should have prevented the conviction of so many people. Gradually, the leaders of society saw the dangers of allowing these safeguards to be trampled over—not just to them, but to the rational ordering of society.

This reassertion of legal safeguards did have a philosophical backdrop. By the end of the seventeenth century, the educated had begun to explore nature in different ways—through science. Some of the "superstitious" beliefs of the past, in angels, devils, and flying witches, were no longer fashionable. Thus the rule of law was properly restored; and one of the grimmest persecutions by Western culture slowly came to an end.

^   A nineteenth-century print of the town of Salem, Massachusetts.

THE MAGIC CIRCLE
AND PENTAGRAM

The magic circle is where rituals and magical workings are
performed. The symbolism of the shape is important—a
circle is endless and infinite, and represents the endless
passage of life, death, and rebirth.

❶ Before a circle is drawn, or "cast," the area is swept away—perhaps with a broom, perhaps by the participants "banishing" negative energies.

❷ The circle is cast with the athame (black-handled knife) or ritual sword in the direction of the movement of the sun (known as deosil). The altar and all the other ritual tools are placed inside the circle.

❸ The circle is then consecrated by invoking the four elements—earth, water, fire, and air. These four elements also correspond to the four quarters of the circle: north, south, east, and west. The correspondences are: north/earth; south/fire; west/water; east/air.

❹ These quarters each have a guardian, the Lords of the Watchtowers, who are then invoked to guard and protect the circle.

❺ This summoning will involve the drawing of a pentagram in the air with an athame. The pentagram is the most important symbol in witchcraft. The exact meaning of the five-pointed star is open to debate. Some believe it represents the four elements plus Man; or plus Spirit; or plus God. Others think it represents the four elements plus "ether," the medium in which witches perform magic. Another view is that the five points represent a human being with his or her arms and legs stretched out. Many witches carry symbols of the pentagram inside a circle or on a circular object—a pentacle.

❻ Once the magic rituals have been completed, witches think it important that the magic circle be properly closed down, and its energies be allowed to dissipate, and that they as people be "earthed" again and connected back to the material world.

THE

MODERN

WORLD

THE

SURVIVAL

The worst excesses of the Burning Times had ended by the beginning of the eighteenth century, but that did not mean witchcraft disappeared entirely from society's consciousness. On the one hand, the traditions of the craft kept alive by the so-called cunning men and wise women have survived through to the twentieth century. Meanwhile, by the nineteenth century, there had emerged a fascination with the occult and magic in Western society that was to have a profound effect on modern-day witchcraft.

OF

WITCHCRAFT

^ At Ilchester, Somerset, in 1871, a local 'wise woman' uses
weird rituals to treat cattle for foot and mouth disease.

Cunning Men, Wise Women

As a result of a new-found quest for reason and rationality—the hallmarks of the Enlightenment—few among the educated elites in the eighteenth century bothered with the superstitions they associated with witchcraft. The dawning of this Age of Reason also shaped views on religion. The God/Devil dichotomy of the Middle Ages, in which the Lord was in daily battle with Satan over people's souls, had been replaced in intellectual minds with a more ordered universe, in which a rational God presided over a rationally explicable order of things.

This was the way of things as described by great writers and philosophers such as Voltaire and Descartes, and later the Scottish philosopher David Hume. There was no room in such a reasonable world for superstitions. This meant that witchcraft, which had stood center stage for hundreds of years as the battleground for this titanic struggle between Good and Evil, now simply vanished from history.

Or at least that was the prevailing view among the ruling elite in Britain, America, and Europe. In the real lives of everyday people, belief in witchcraft and its powers persisted. Such a belief rarely linked magic with the Devil. Instead, people instinctively accepted that certain men or women had powers and secret knowledge, and were to be respected or feared—or often a mixture of both. These people were known as cunning men or wise women. They had existed before the Burning Times, had somehow survived during those times' persecutions, and were now still to be found throughout much of Western Europe and North America.

Healing Powers

Some cunning men or wise women had indeed been tried and executed as witches, though there is evidence to suggest that they were often able to avoid persecution—in part because of the respect in which they were held in communities and the valued services they provided. But many survived, and during the eighteenth and nineteenth centuries were able to practice their craft without serious risk of prosecution in many parts of Europe and America. It is their survival that, in a sense, provides the one tangible continuity between the modern day and the ancient practices of witchcraft tradition.

Recent research by modern historians such as Owen Davies and Ronald Hutton has thrown a great deal of light upon the work, beliefs, and status of the cunning folk, especially in Britain. In particular, it appears that they were distinguished in the minds of ordinary people from "witches," who, though they had the same or similar occult powers, practiced them malevolently. In fact, one of the primary roles of the cunning folk seems to have been to help people who had been cursed by "witches."

However, this is not to say that some people who were generally regarded as cunning folk—and therefore "good"—could not be regarded as malevolent by a minority. As ever in the history of witchcraft, perception was everything.

There were, interestingly, more males than females among the cunning folk. The men generally practiced their witchcraft as a secondary job in addition to their main employment, while for women it was their only source of income. As well as the terms "cunning" or "wise" folk, men were known as "wizards" or "conjurors." They were also known as "dyn hysbys" in Wales, and called a "peller" in Cornwall in southwest England. Some even took the title "Doctor" to lend themselves more respectability. In parts of North America, such people were variously described as witch masters, white witches, witch doctors, power doctors, and conjure folk.

One of the main functions of the cunning folk was that of healer and diviner, as well as helping lift curses. Their advice was sought on matters of love, the fortunes of harvest, poor health, the finding of treasure, and such. The wise woman or cunning man might provide herbal remedies, creams to help remove warts, or good-luck charms. And, contrary to popular belief, they were often to be found in towns as well as rural areas.

∧ A witch feeding her familiars – two toads and a cat – with her own
blood, taken from the 1579 pamphlet "A Rehearsal Both Strange and True"
detailing the actions of 65-year-old Elizabeth Stile from Windsor, England,
and three others accused of witchcraft.

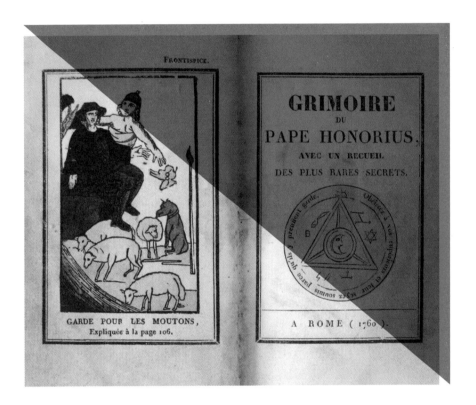

∧ The *Grimoire of Pope Honorius* is an eighteenth-century book of spells claiming to have been written by Pope Honorius III (1150–1227)

Magical Books

The tools of a wise woman or man included crystals for scrying, divining rods, wands, swords, knives, and books. Their libraries included the Bible, which was often used as an oracle, and grimoires (books of spells and rituals), plus publications on the tarot, astrology, and fortune-telling. The written word was felt to contain power, and these magical books took on a supernatual power.

As well as owning books, some cunning folk created their own books on a variety of subjects, including astrology, herbal medicine, and magical spells. Many of the practitioners used the books to record their practices, their ideas, and any useful information they may have gleaned from elsewhere. In modern witchcraft the equivalent for a witch is known as a Book of Shadows.

It cannot be presumed that cunning folk subscribed to one universal set of beliefs. They were practitioners of an ancient craft passed down from person to person or taught by those with a particular calling to it, rather than as keepers of a particular faith. From the surviving books they have left behind, it would appear that they could invoke in their spells a wide variety of entities, including Christian saints, angels, fairies, and the Holy Trinity. There is no surviving record of a cunning person that suggests that he or she specifically invoked a pagan deity, though of course this does not mean it did not happen.

Lynch Mobs

It would be misleading to suggest that the eighteenth and nineteenth centuries were times of complete peace and harmony as far as witchcraft is concerned. It is true that legislation in Britain in 1736, for example, repealed and replaced the earlier English and Scottish witchcraft laws. And it is also the case that few, if any, people were prosecuted in the eighteenth century in Britain under these new laws, which were aimed at those who falsely claimed they were working magic.

However, ordinary people who were fearful of magical powers, and who believed they had been victims of witchcraft, could and did take the law into their own hands, rather than employ the services of a "friendly" witch. The difference now, though, was that the rule of law—which was gradually strengthening throughout Western societies as they themselves became more centralized—meant that the perpetrators of the attacks were now the ones prosecuted.

This is illustrated by the case of an elderly couple from Hertfordshire, England, in 1751. The pair were suspected of witchcraft and dragged from their home to be plunged into water—the familiar medieval test for a witch. When the couple floated back to the surface they were deemed guilty, pulled out, and beaten to death by the mob. The ringleader of the group responsible was later hanged for murder.

Cunning Murrell

During the nineteenth century there were also a number of prosecutions under the previously mentioned 1736 Act. And, in 1824, the Vagrancy Act made it illegal to use "any subtle craft, means and device . . . to deceive and impose" and was intended to ban practices such as palmistry and fortune-telling, among other things. However, studies of those prosecutions that were brought against cunning folk suggest they were not really state-inspired attacks on witchcraft. Instead, many of them were inspired by disgruntled clients who felt they had been duped or overcharged, while some cases were brought against clear fraudsters who were masquerading as cunning folk.

One of the best-documented cunning men of the period was James Murrell (1780–1860) from the village of Hadleigh, in Essex, England. Cunning Murrell, as he was known, was an eccentric character, who

∧ A woodcut showing a witch hanging in England in the
seventeenth century.

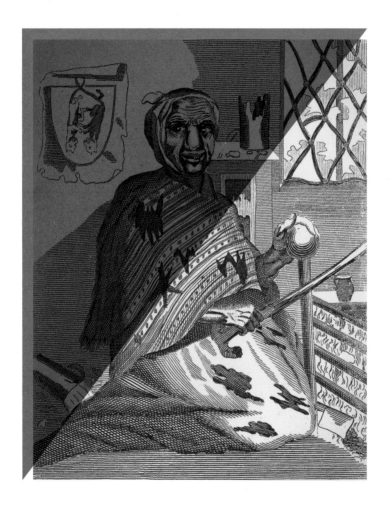

∧ A portrait of Jinny Bingham, also known as Mother
Damnable, the Shrew of Kentish Town, and other names,
who was reputedly a practitioner of magic.

THE SURVIVAL OF WITCHCRAFT

used to wander at night wearing metal goggles, sporting a tail coat, and carrying a whalebone umbrella whatever the weather, humming loudly as he went and apparently deep in contemplation. He had a wide list of clients, and offered to cure warts and other ailments such as gout and impotence, and to retrieve stolen property. But his main reputation came from his reputed ability to lift curses that had been put on people by other witches. Murrell liked to claim that he was "the Devil's master." Like many leading cunning men of his time, Murrell kept in frequent contact with people and events in London, where many prominent occultists lived, and was a respected, if sometimes feared, member of the community.

The existence of the cunning folk continued on into the twentieth century and does so even to this day. Yet their precise legacy to modern-day witchcraft is not entirely clear. It is apparent that the cunning folk did not, and do not, see themselves as part of an "Old Religion," or indeed any religion at all. Yet some modern practitioners of Witchcraft or Wicca—which is a mystery-based religion—do still draw on the tradition of the cunning folk as an inspiration for their own practices. The cunning folk are, for them, an important link to the past. As we shall see, the origins of modern Wicca are complex and controversial. To understand those origins more clearly, it is first necessary to examine other trends in Western society during the eighteenth and nineteenth centuries.

The Romantic Age

While the cunning folk were keeping witchcraft alive in one area of society during the eighteenth and nineteenth centuries, the perception of witchcraft and magic by the educated elite underwent a transformation over the same 200 years.

Initially, witchcraft and magic were largely neglected in intellectual circles: Science and the new rational philosophies excited people's interest instead. However, the start of the nineteenth century and the beginnings of the Romantic era heralded a new fascination with the subject in many parts of continental Europe.

In Germany, Karl Ernst Jarcke first suggested that witchcraft had an ancient past, as part of a nature religion practiced by the German people. By 1862 a French writer, Jules Michelet, was claiming that witchcraft had been a protest movement against feudalism and aristocratic oppression, and that these protestors had used the remains of an ancient fertility rite to express their anger. Though this analysis hardly stands even a cursory examination of witch trials during the Burning Times, Michelet's view about the fertility cult became influential in nineteenth-century writings.

At the same time, a Frenchman calling himself Éliphas Lévi (his real name was Alphonse Louis Constant) was reviving interest in ritual magic. Lévi was born a Catholic in 1810, and died one in 1875, but in between became fascinated by magic and produced a number of highly influential books on the subject, including *The Dogma and Ritual of High Magic*, *A History of Magic*, and *The Key of Great Mysteries*. The distinction of Lévi's work was the manner in which it linked different secret traditions and provided a continuity of belief and practice with the past. His work linked the Knights Templar, Egyptian mythology, and the Holy Grail. His study of the Kabbalah and the tarot provided a blueprint for ritual magic in the modern age.

In particular, Lévi's use of the expression "High Magic" signified an elevated blending of the practical and mystical aspects of magic. Lévi's trailblazing work was taken on by others, many of them Freemasons and/ or Rosicrucians. These were secret societies that had been popular from the eighteenth century across Europe.

By 1888 Lévi's ideas gained concrete expression in a new occult organization founded in Britain, called the Hermetic Order of the Golden Dawn. Dedicated to the philosophical, spiritual, and psychic evolution of humanity, its members practiced astral travel, studied the Kabbalah, and read tarot cards. Its core was ritual magic which was to provide this mystical union between the human spirit and the divine.

∧ Jules Michelet (1798–1874) was an influential French
historian and writer.

One of its leading members for a period was the controversial magician Aleister Crowley, who in turn influenced Gerald Gardner, the man who was to have such an impact on witchcraft in the twentieth century.

Italian Witches

Meanwhile, an American folklore expert and journalist, Charles Leland, had published a book called *Aradia, or the Gospel of the Witches* in 1899. This popular volume described his meetings with an Italian witch named Maddalena, who then introduced him to other witches. Leland picked up the idea from Michelet that witches had been a protest movement against feudalism, and also stated that the Italian tradition to which Maddalena belonged had revered the goddess Diana as its chief deity. Diana, said the witches, was the first witch of the Vecchia Religione, the "Old Religion." Leland's theories were supported by the books of the Egyptologist Margaret Murray, who published *The Witch Cult in Western Europe*, in 1921, and later *The God of the Witches*.

Murray's thesis was that there had been a fertility cult in Europe up to the seventeenth century, which had a horned god as its main deity. In her view, the Burning Times signaled the final defeat of this ancient cult at the hands of the Christian hierarchy, who were determined to remove the "Old Religion" from Europe once and for all. This cult, she claimed, had been organized into covens of thirteen witches.

Murray's scholarship in these books, and her romantic portrayal of a surviving fertility cult in Western Europe, has since been widely discredited by academics. But her views were to catch the public imagination, especially after the end of World War II. In doing so, they helped form an important backdrop to the emergence of modern witchcraft in the twentieth century.

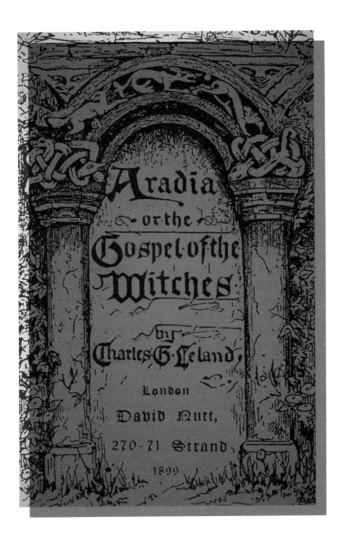

∧ Charles Leland's *Aradia, or the Gospel of Witches,* was published in 1899 and was influential in establishing the goddess Diana as the chief deity revered by witches.

THE

BIRTH

Wicca, the name usually given to the modern practice of witchcraft, is a fast-growing religion with followers in many parts of the world. Like all religions, it has a foundation story; and, as with most religions, this foundation story is shrouded in controversy and uncertainty. However, what is not in doubt is the central role of one man in developing this modern form of pagan witchcraft—Gerald Gardner.

OF

WICCA

The Civil Servant: Gerald Gardner

When the religion of Wicca emerged in Britain in the early 1950s, its early adherents maintained that it was a direct, surviving descendant of an ancient fertility cult which had worshipped a goddess and a horned god, and that this tradition had lasted through the dark days of the Burning Times and been preserved in one or two covens in England. This view dovetailed perfectly with the published opinions of Charles Leland, the American folklorist, and Margaret Murray, the British Egyptologist, whose works were widely accepted at the time.

This concept of a surviving tradition of a pagan witchcraft religion has since been widely challenged, to the point where few practicing witches subscribe to it. But, initially, this dramatic re-emergence of the "Old Religion" struck a chord with many who believed—or wanted to believe—the wonderfully romantic history provided by Leland and Murray.

Gerald Brosseau Gardner may appear on the surface an unlikely person to be credited with the development—or creation—of such a religion. He was born on June 13, 1884, to a reasonably wealthy family near Liverpool in northwest England, and spent much of his life abroad, working in the Far East, both in the private sector running tea or rubber plantations in Borneo and Malaya; then working for the British authorities as an official in the customs service in Malaya (now within Malaysia).

Gardner had not undergone a university education but had developed a passion for archeology, folklore history, and anthropology. He was also interested in spiritual matters, including religion, magic, and the occult, subjects he read on widely. These were interests that were to stand him in good stead when it came to the development of the Wicca religion.

Gardner retired in 1936 from his service abroad and returned to England, first to London, then to a beautiful area of southern England known as the New Forest. It was in this rural idyll, Gardner later claimed, that events occurred that were to have a profound effect not just on him, but on the future of modern witchcraft.

∧ Gerald Gardner, the founder of modern-day Wicca, is depicted here with a number of symbols derived from the Italian pagan tradition.

∧ A nineteenth-century engraving of the New Forest. It was here that Gerald Gardner joined a coven whose beliefs formed the basis for Gardnerian Wicca.

New Forest Coven

Of all the controversies surrounding the origins of Wicca, one of the most crucial hinges on the existence, or otherwise, of a coven of witches in the New Forest area. Gardner was later to claim that he discovered the existence of the old witch religion when he was initiated into such a coven in September 1939—the month that war was declared in Europe.

Gardner claimed that he was initiated into the coven in 1939 by a wealthy woman, whose name was Old Dorothy Clutterbuck. One interesting story that Gardner later told about Old Dorothy took place in 1940, when Britain felt under impending threat from a Nazi invasion. According to Gardner, Old Dorothy convened a meeting of different covens from around the country, who all met in the New Forest. This group cast a great circle and raised a witches' "cone of power" directed at Hitler and his troops, which said, "Do not come." A number of these witches, who were quite elderly, supposedly died a few days later from their exertions. There was, incidentally, a tradition that a similar cone of power had been raised by English witches against the invasion force of the Spanish Armada in 1588, which was ultimately defeated with the help of freak weather conditions.

Aleister Crowley

Soon after the end of World War II, Gardner met Aleister Crowley. Crowley's reputation as the "Wickedest Man in the World" came from his own entertaining utterances about himself, and his encouragement of publicity about him by others. Crowley certainly was a powerful character who still has many followers within the world of magic, and this meeting between the two men has attracted much speculation. At this time Crowley, by now an old man with just a short time left to live, was the head of the Ordo Templi Orientis (OTO), a society established in Germany which was influenced by a number of sources, including mystical Freemasonry, the work of the Frenchman Éliphas Lévi, and various ancient traditions.

The meetings between Gardner and Crowley encouraged the former to revive the work of the OTO in Britain and create a new section. Indeed, upon Crowley's death in 1947, members of the OTO apparently assumed that Gardner would take over as its head in Europe, though Gardner's attempts to start a new section soon petered out.

This link between Gardner and Crowley at a crucial time in the emergence of the Wicca movement has led to much discussion and debate. Some adherents of Crowley claimed that the magician's encouragement of Gardner to found a new organization (albeit within the OTO framework) means that Crowley became, in effect, the father of modern witchcraft.

This argument seems to fall down on several grounds. During his life Crowley made relatively few references to witchcraft, and those that he did make were not sympathetic. Also, Crowley preferred the rituals and practice of "high" magic, which was reflected in his membership in the Hermetic Order of the Golden Dawn and latterly the OTO, and seemed less interested in religion.

More convincing is the argument that Crowley has had an influence on some of the ritualistic content of Wicca, through his own prolific and powerful writings.

In the 1940s, Gardner was collating material that was eventually to make up his collection of rituals and beliefs, which would stand at the heart of the new witchcraft religion. This book was to become known as *The Book of Shadows* (see page 200). He was also preparing a novel called *High Magic's Aid*, which appeared in 1949 and showed within it the combination of high ceremonial magic, paganism, and witchcraft, and was to be a hallmark of the Wicca movement.

The influences moving Gardner in this direction were several. One was his interest in high or ceremonial magic, through his meetings with Crowley, his membership in the OTO, and his interest in Masonic rituals.

∧ English writer and occultist Aleister Crowley (1875–1947)
was interested in the rituals and practice of "high" magic.

∧ The Ancient Order of Druids, which enhanced Gerald Gardner's interest
in rituals and paganism, is the oldest druidic order still in existence.

Another was his interest in the work of Margaret Murray, whom he knew from their membership in the Folklore Society in Britain, and whose theories about the ancient fertility cults of Europe have already been mentioned. Gardner was also by 1946 a member of the governing council of the Ancient Order of Druids, the most active mystical Druidic group of the period.

At the same time, Gardner had helped recreate a sixteenth-century witches' cottage on land near St. Albans, Hertfordshire, England, and by the early 1950s was involved in a coven based there; whether this was the continuation of a New Forest coven or was a newly established group is unclear.

The repeal in 1951 of the last remaining anti-witchcraft legislation in Britain, the Witchcraft and Vagrancy Acts, effectively freed people to practice witchcraft without fear of prosecution. Thus from 1951 a series of newspaper articles appeared—partly inspired by Gardner—that discussed the presence of witchcraft in Britain. These articles, initially, were relatively positive about the practice, stressing the middle-class nature of the participants and the desire of witches to do good.

This tentative publicity was followed in 1954 with the publication of Gardner's book *Witchcraft Today*, in which he announced to the world that the religion of witchcraft was alive and had survived from ancient times, and that he called it "Wicca," though he initially spelled it with a single "c"—"Wica." "Wicca" meant a male witch in Old English, "wicce" a female one. Wicca was formerly pronounced "witch-ah" but is now pronounced with a hard "c" as "wick-ah."

Gardner's *Witchcraft Today* was written from the point of view of a disinterested anthropologist, and described some of its rituals, including a midwinter ceremony. It positioned the "Myth of the Goddess" as the "Central Theme of Witchcraft," and reverence for the Goddess remains one of the essential tenets of Wiccan belief and practice.

With the publication of *Witchcraft Today*, then, the modern concept of a witchcraft religion had emerged.

The Role of Doreen Valiente

The person who helped Gardner develop much of the detail and tone of the religion in the 1950s was Doreen Valiente. She had been initiated into Gardner's coven in 1953, and quickly established herself as a powerful creative force—in time she was to become the coven's high priestess. Valiente, who died in 1999 and was an acclaimed writer on witchcraft, was encouraged by Gardner to develop the rituals of the coven. The two of them in particular helped to rewrite material that was to appear in Gardner's grimoire (book of rituals and spells). He was later to call this *The Book of Shadows*, and it was and remains the repository of information on the religion's beliefs and practices. Gradually the pair removed much of the Christian imagery from the early material, which had been strongly influenced by Masonic and Rosicrucian writings.

Valiente also pointed out to Gardner that much of the material in the coven's rituals borrowed heavily from Aleister Crowley, whose writings included *Liber AL vel Legis* (Book of the Law), and the Gnostic Mass. Gardner told her that this was because the material he had been given by the New Forest coven had been fragmentary, and he had needed to supplement much of that with other writings—including those of Crowley—which he felt caught the mood and meaning of the religion's beliefs and practices. Valiente wrote some of this and in the course of her rewriting of various materials, she produced a new version of the "Charge of the Goddess," which remains to this day one of the central tenets of Wiccan belief and spirituality. This "charge" is a poetic incantation given by the Goddess through her intermediary, the high priestess of the coven.

Valiente and Gardner were eventually to fall out over the key question of publicity for the religion. Gardner's view, as expressed to Valiente, was that he needed to publicize the "Old Religion" because its members were elderly (as he himself was by then) and they needed to attract new people. This, incidentally, was what had happened with Valiente

∧ Image taken from *The Mirror of Wisdom of the Rosicrucians*, a text written in 1618. Gardner's early writings on Wicca were influenced by this spiritual movement.

∧ Traditionally, cunning folk or wise women often used
tarot as a method for fortune-telling. Image from *The
Illustrated Key To The Tarot The Veil Of Divination* (1916)
by L.W. de Laurence.

herself, who was attracted to join in 1952 by reading about Wicca in a newspaper article.

But Valiente and her followers were unhappy at the kind of lurid headlines that Gardner and witchcraft had been attracting in sections of the British media. Some of this specifically linked (with no supporting evidence) the practice of witches with worship of the Devil—a very emotive throwback to the days of the Burning Times.

In her 1973 book *An ABC of Witchcraft Past and Present*, Valiente sets out her views. "There is no doubt that [Gardner's] action was a complete break with the whole witch tradition of silence and secrecy . . . Today, many persons inside the witch cult regard [Gardner] as having done more harm than good by his publication of witchcraft."

The rift over publicity became a break in 1957. Valiente's faction in the coven drafted a set of thirteen proposed rules for the craft, including a commitment to secrecy. Gardner's response was to produce a set of "Laws of the Craft" which, though written in archaic language, were fairly obviously his invention. The Valiente faction went off to form a separate coven.

Spreading the Net

Though the fledging Wicca movement was now suffering some internal dissent, there was still no shortage of potential recruits wanting to come forward to be initiated into the new "Old" religion. This was perhaps partly due to the publicity that Gardner and his new high priestess, known as Dayonis, continued to attract. Such publicity was, as is always the case with publicity, a double-edged sword. Though it did reveal to the public the existence of a religion whose main tenets included a reverence for nature, a desire to help the world, and a sense of continuity with humankind's past, there were enough negative images, too, to deter people. For example, while Gardner put great emphasis on the fact that rituals were performed naked (or "sky-clad") to symbolize the freedom of those involved, it was predictably seized upon by some journalists as a sign of "depravity."

The positive side was evidenced by the number of high priestesses whom Gardner himself initiated from 1957 after contacting the coven, and who went on themselves to found covens in different parts of the country, including London, Yorkshire, Lancashire, and Scotland. This undoubtedly helped in the spread of the Wicca movement throughout the 1960s and 1970s.

On the other hand, the danger of the publicity was demonstrated in 1959, when a British tabloid newspaper, which had earlier been given access to the Gardner coven in return for an agreement to write a sympathetic article, printed the names, addresses, and photographs of the members.

This public "outing" forced the coven to let it be known to other journalists that they had disbanded, while in reality they had quietly moved to another location.

Rival Traditions

By the time of Gardner's death in early 1964, the Gardnerian Tradition (as it came to be called) of Wicca had evolved quite fully. The movement was characterized by a union of the vivid paganism popular in the nineteenth and twentieth centuries in Europe and the historical concept of the witch—in line with the views of Leland and Murray. This worked well with the folk tradition of the cunning men and wise women, the people who had kept a form of witchcraft practice alive over hundreds of years.

Meanwhile, instead of a monotheistic system, Gardner's polytheistic tradition extolled the virtues of a Horned God and, increasingly, the central importance of the Goddess at the heart of the religion. The

∧ Charles Leland (1824–1903) was an American poet and folklore expert whose work *Aradia, or the Gospel of Witches,* was published in 1899.

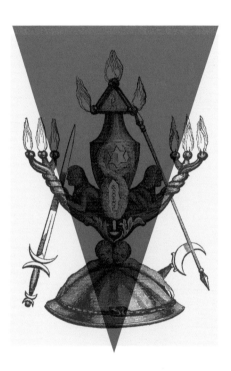

∧ French occultist Éliphas Lévi's writings have had a strong influence on popular occult thought since the late nineteenth century, especially so on tarot design. The symbols used here are from the 1896 English version of Lévi's *Transcendental Magic: Its Doctrine and Ritual*.

Wiccan rituals emphasized the importance of the polarity between these two in nature, as well as their symbolic union.

Another key element was the acknowledgment of the "north" in rituals, which was associated with darkness, and thus rejected by those traditions—such as Freemasonry—that were associated with Christianity. Under Gardner, the north and its darkness was not something to be feared but to be embraced as one crucial part of the essential whole circle of the universe. Gardnerian witchcraft also came to champion the role of women in rituals, as the high priestess took over the senior role in covens. The action of the priestess in "Drawing Down the Moon," that is becoming, in effect, the Goddess herself, is at the heart of the mystery of Wiccan belief.

Another crucial aspect of the religion was that would-be members had to be initiated into the tradition, normally by the opposite gender. The initiation took place inside a magic circle, and there were three degrees of initiation, each one revealing progressively more secret knowledge to the initiate—an idea familiar in Masonry and other secret societies. The Third Degree was the highest, most adept level.

However, the loose, almost haphazard development of Gardner's fledgling "movement" in the late 1950s and early 1960s was not a recipe for uniformity, and it was perhaps inevitable that other, rival traditions would soon emerge. The most important of these early rival approaches was to be the Alexandrian tradition of Wicca, which was created by Alexander Sanders (1926–88). Born in Manchester in the northwest of England, Sanders was initiated into the Gardnerian movement, but, after Gardner's death, Sanders claimed he had been initiated as a child by his grandmother from another tradition altogether.

Sanders was a flamboyant character, the self-styled "King of the Witches," who assiduously courted publicity and attracted notoriety and became, with his partner Maxine, well known in Britain during the 1960s. Though Sanders was responsible for some lurid publicity for witchcraft, and alienated even some of those he had initiated into the craft, his powerful personality and distinct practices did help develop a unique tradition. The Alexandrian tradition developed by Sanders put more emphasis on the ceremonial ritual of "high" magic than Gardner had, and reflected the work of Éliphas Lévi. Sanders also championed the use of practical magical techniques such as astral projection, clairvoyance, and the use of talismans and charms.

Creation or Discovery?

So what is the true role of Gerald Gardner in relation to modern Wicca? The evidence certainly indicates that this retired colonial administrator from England did not "discover" a witchcraft religion that had somehow gone unnoticed for hundreds of years. It turns out that he is not a discoverer, but a creator, or perhaps it is better to say a recreator of the pagan religion. By drawing together strands of nineteenth-century belief about paganism and the history of witchcraft, and combining it with both the ceremonial high magic of the eighteenth, nineteenth, and twentieth centuries, plus the "low" magic of traditional witchcraft, Gardner came up with something new and distinct. In this context, the "foundation" story of Wicca may be less important than it seems.

As with any religion, it is the content and how it evolves that count, more than where it came from. And, in Gardner's case, the success of Wicca today suggests that he recreated something new and important.

^ Taken from Lévi's *Transcendental Magic: Its Doctrine and Ritual*, on the left is the Seal of Solomon, or intersecting triangles of light and darkness, and on the right is the sign of excommunication, projecting a shadow of a demon.

COVENS

A coven is the traditional name given to a group of witches who perform rituals and magic together. Covens are historically supposed to have thirteen members, though the origins of this are unclear. Nowadays there are many covens with fewer than thirteen members—or coveners—and some feel that having more than thirteen makes the coven too unwieldy.

High Priestess and High Priest

The leader of the coven is nearly always the high priestess. The high priestess works closely with the high priest in a partnership but, though they share some leadership responsibilities, it is she who ultimately is the head of the coven. Many high priestesses tend to view this position as "first among equals." In the end, though, it is her responsibility to ensure that the coven is harmonious and that the personalities involved blend together in a unified way.

Every other member of the coven—apart from these two—is a priestess or priest. Many covens also designate one experienced priestess as the "maiden." Her job may entail substituting sometimes for the high priestess, to assist in training, or to allot tasks such as cleaning or administration to other members of the coven. Another position, traditionally carried out by a man, is that of "fetch," who works as a kind of messenger and envoy to the high priestess.

Witchcraft is not an evangelical religion and potential recruits cannot simply expect to join any coven they want. The coven will vet any candidates to ensure they are suitable. The recruits are trained— traditionally this period is for a year and a day. If they are suitable, and fit in with the values and personalities of the coven, they are initiated into the group. There are three degrees of initiation, with the Third Degree being the highest level—the level at which you are entitled to be a high priestess or high priest. A new coven may be formed by a Third-Degree couple "hiving off" to start one.

WICCA

The Wiccan tradition arrived in the United States in the 1960s, and America now has more followers of the Wiccan religion than anywhere else in the world.

GOES

The arrival of Wicca built on the traditions of witchcraft in the country, but really exploded in popularity after combining with another potent force: feminism.

WEST

∧ From c.1913, a mountain woman sits at a spinning wheel;
some areas of the U.S. remained isolated and remote
well into the twentieth century, and belief in witchcraft
remained a prominent part of these communities.

Origins of Witchcraft in the U.S.

The horrors of the witch craze in the United States in the seventeenth and eighteenth centuries were not the end of that story of witchcraft in America.

In 1947 the folklore expert Vince Randolph published a book called *Ozark Superstitions*, which was based on lengthy research he had carried out early in the twentieth century in the Ozark uplands of Arkansas and Missouri. Randolph spent a long time with the people who lived in this remote, isolated location, and described how they had had little contact with the outside world for a hundred years. Many of the families could trace their lineage directly back to families from England and Scotland who had come over in early colonial times. Randolph recorded many of their stories and beliefs, a prominent part of which was in the real presence of witches and witchcraft in their communities.

One of the interesting points that come from Randolph's research is that the American communities made clear distinctions between "good" witches, whom they called "witch masters," and "bad" witches. This outlook mirrors the manner in which European societies differentiated between the "cunning folk" and malevolent witches.

According to the people of the Ozarks, the bad witches enjoyed stealing milk and preventing butter from forming. They also took the shape of any animal or bird, and caused illness or even death among members of the community. Randolph described the methods used by locals to protect themselves. Nailing crosses of hazel wood on to their buildings was a popular way to ward off the effects of bad witches. The ultimate option, however, was to call in a professional—a witch master. Their many techniques included making a beeswax image or "poppet" of the suspected witch, covering it in cloth worn by the suspect, and then burning it or driving nails into it.

Little subsequent research was done to verify these claims, and, considering the fact that the interviews took place around one hundred years ago, the trail has gone cold. Yet Randolph's study reveals a surviving, low-level tradition of witchcraft in America, bearing a slim resemblance to the beliefs that form the modern-day religion of Wicca.

Raymond Buckland

Nevertheless, there can be little doubt that the origins of the modern Wicca movement in the U.S. stem, like those in Britain, from the activities of one man: in this case Raymond Buckland. Buckland was born in London, England, in 1934, and as a child soon developed an interest in spiritualism. He was in the Royal Air Force until 1959 before moving to live in the United States in 1962. By then, Buckland was already deeply interested in witchcraft and had been corresponding with Gerald Gardner for some time. In 1963 Buckland and his wife Rosemary flew to Perth, Scotland, to meet Gardner, where he was trained and then initiated into the Wiccan tradition by one of Gardner's own initiates, Monique Wilson. Rosemary Buckland was initiated at a later date. The pair returned to the United States armed with the Gardnerian *Book of Shadows*, and later that year founded the New York coven in Bay Shore on Long Island. Rosemary Buckland took on the magical name of Lady Rowen and assumed the role of high priestess.

The Wiccan religion had formally arrived in the United States.

Buckland also became Gardner's spokesperson in America, and the coven ran on very similar lines to those of a Gardnerian tradition in Britain. For well over ten years, Buckland and his New York coven were at the center of the Wicca religion in the United States, and to this day, most "official" Gardnerian covens in the U.S. can trace their heritage from that original group.

The Buckland coven, however, came under criticism for what was considered its too cautious approach to accepting new members. The 1960s was a time of great spiritual awareness and awakenings, and people

∧ An artistic representation of a twentieth century
Witches' Sabbat from 1927.

∧ An all-seeing eye inside a triple moon—a Wiccan moon goddess symbol.

wanted to experience new practices, ways of life, and belief structures. This put Buckland and his wife under increasing pressure to initiate people more quickly, and with less training than they would have liked.

To an extent, there was a clash of cultures developing. The Bucklands came from the Gardnerian tradition, which was the product of postwar Britain of the 1940s and 1950s, a society that was conservative and inward-looking. The America of the 1960s was very different, thanks to the emergence of the so-called counterculture. Therefore, those who were unable to be absorbed into Wicca through the New York Gardnerian coven could, and did, find other ways into witchcraft, establishing their own covens and practices.

Seax-Wica

Major changes began to occur in the New York coven within a decade of its foundation. In 1972 Rosemary Buckland stood down as high priestess, and a new pair, Theos and Phoenix, took over as high priestess and high priest respectively, moving the coven to Commack in Suffolk County, Long Island, at the same time. With the help of Rosemary Buckland, the coven now drew up a list of "Notes and Guidance" to add to the Gardnerian *Book of Shadows*. The marriage of the Bucklands ended by 1973, and Raymond Buckland left the New York coven just ten years after he had founded it.

Nevertheless, Raymond Buckland was still to play an important role in the development of witchcraft in America. By 1969 he had published his first major book, *A Pocket Guide to the Supernatural*, and two years later wrote one of his best-known works, *Witchcraft from the Inside*.

In 1973, Buckland created the Seax-Wica tradition of Wicca. It is based heavily on Saxon heritage, and does not have strict rules on secrecy or the immutability of rituals. It also differs from Gardnerian Wicca in allowing people to become self-initiated, rather than having to be initiated by an existing member. Buckland's 1974 book *The Tree: Complete Book of Saxon Witchcraft* set out the beliefs of Seax-Wica.

Back in New York, the Gardnerian coven continued to initiate more people into the highest degree of initiation—the Third Degree—and these people in turn went off and established their own covens all over the United States. In 1973 there were roughly thirty Gardnerian covens in the U.S., a number that was to increase rapidly in the coming years.

New covens sprang up all over the country, some directly Gardnerian, some unofficial offshoots, others still claiming entirely different roots. As in Britain, there were some covens that claimed "traditional" heritage— that is, an ancient lineage of practicing witchcraft that predated the Wicca religion. Some American witches also disliked what they saw as the overly hierarchical structures of covens "imported" from Britain.

Once in America, then, witchcraft had moved beyond the narrow confines of its British roots and began to sprout an incredible variety of practices and beliefs, which, though still essentially Wiccan, were constantly evolving. And one of the main influences on this process of evolution of Wicca in the U.S. was feminism.

Feminism and Witchcraft

It is hard to overemphasize the importance of feminism in its influence on Wicca first in America, then in the rest of the world. In effect, Wicca became the spiritual dimension of feminism, while feminism strengthened Wicca's social and political identity. The combination of these two activations was to transform the nature of modern witchcraft.

An early indication of how feminism might dovetail with witchcraft came in 1968 with the formation of the short-lived organization WITCH—the Women's International Terrorist Conspiracy from Hell. It stated, among many other things, that witches during the Middle Ages and early modern period had been subjected to oppression by a male elite,

∧ The sprial Goddess is a modern Wiccan symbol
representing the creative powers of the Divine Feminine,
and the never-ending circle of creation.

∧ American women's rights advocate, writer, and editor,
Matilda Joslyn Gage (1826–98).

and that nine million witches, an overwhelming majority of them female, had been killed as a direct result.

This was not an entirely new theory. Jules Michelet argued as early as 1862 that the medieval witches were fighting, unsuccessfully, against oppressive feudalism, an idea adopted by some Marxists. Charles Leland had also explored this issue. More relevantly still, at the end of the nineteenth century, the extraordinary, pioneering American feminist Matilda Joslyn Gage had seen the witch hunts in terms of a persecution of female spiritual leadership.

Nonetheless, this re-presented theory resonated powerfully in the context of the modern Wicca movement, which alone of religions sought to highlight female spirituality in the form of the Goddess.

By the mid 1970s, writers of the stature of Mary Daly and Andrea Dworkin were incorporating the history of witchcraft into their thesis of how women's power had first been supplanted and then forcibly repressed in society. In this way, the Burning Times were seen by feminist writers as exemplifying the battle of women against the patriarchal elements of society throughout history.

Spirituality

The feminist critique of the 1970s, therefore, helped to put Wicca and its beliefs in a modern social context. However, many of these writers were far more interested in those social and political aspects than they were in the spiritual side of Wicca. That spiritual context was provided, in part, by the Hungarian-born feminist Z. Budapest, who moved to the U.S. at the end of the 1950s. Budapest, whose own mother was a medium and witch, and whose grandmother had been an herbalist and healer, established her own coven in California in 1971. It was named the Susan B. Anthony Coven Number 1, in honor of the renowned nineteenth-century campaigner for female suffrage.

In time, this coven initiated some 700 women and led to the formation of other, similar covens around the U.S. In 1975, Budapest published *The Feminist Book of Lights and Shadows* (later republished as *The Holy Book of Women's Mysteries*), which found a huge following. The Budapest practices were based on traditional Wicca, but with a decided focus upon feminine and aggressive elements. Witches were encouraged to fight patriarchal oppression and to regain power over their own souls. They were to connect directly with the goddess spirit of the universe and with themselves. This new form of Wicca, with its emphasis on the Goddess, was to become known as the Dianic Tradition, after the classical goddess of the moon and of the hunt, Diana. It was part of a major explosion of interest in witchcraft in the 1970s and early 1980s. It is not hard to see the reasons why. The Dianic tradition was one way for women to express their spirituality other than in the confines of a traditionally male-oriented Christian Church.

Another important figure in the development of witchcraft and feminism was Starhawk (real name Miriam Simos), who published her hugely popular book *The Spiral Dance: A Rebirth of the Ancient Religion of the Great Goddess* in 1979—a work widely credited with bringing many new people to the craft. Starhawk, a writer of great poetic ability, linked the spiritual development of individuals and society through witchcraft with political engagement on such issues as the environment and social justice. Her work, though still strongly feminist in nature, also helped bridge the gap between feminist witchcraft and men involved in Wicca, who were excluded from some forms of the Dianic tradition.

Feminism was not the only driving force toward diversity in modern American witchcraft. The Faeries had most definitely had their part. It was the Feri Tradition (formerly called Faery) established by Victor Anderson and Gwydion Pendderwen, which initiated Starhawk into witchcraft.

In turn Anderson was initiated at the age of nine in Oregon during the early part of the twentieth century. His teachers described themselves

∧ Diana, the goddess of childbirth and women's rites of passage is depicted with the new moon on her head and a cape embroidered with stars.

as "faeries," and revered the "Old Powers," as they called them, but had no formal theology. In this way the faeries were similar to the cunning folk of Britain, and find more evidence supporting a folk tradition of witchcraft in the United States. According to *The Encyclopaedia of Witches and Witchcraft*, written by Rosemary Ellen Guiley, most of the witches Anderson worked with were from the South. Their approach was essentially a "devotional science," and they followed a way of life that laid emphasis on harmony with nature. Anderson and Pendderwen later incorporated parts of the Alexandrian tradition into Feri practices after the latter became acquainted with witches in Britain.

We have seen how modern Wicca religion had arrived in America at the start of the 1960s as a theologically radical but socially conservative movement. Within the space of two decades this had been transformed, revolutionized, and diversified into the pluralistic religion that is Wicca today, both in America and, increasingly, the rest of the world. At the heart of this transformation was feminism. The link between women demanding equal rights and standing in society on the one hand, and the core message of Wicca that saw female spirituality at the heart of the universe on the other, was to prove irresistible.

The Charge of the Goddess

There are many different versions of 'The Charge of the Goddess', which is attributed to Doreen Valiente. This is a section of one version.

Listen to the words from the Great Mother, who was of old called amongst men, Isis, Artemis, Astarte, Dione, Melusine, Aphrodite, Diana, Arionrhod, and by many other names.

Whenever you have need of anything, once in the month and better it be when the Moon is full or new, then shall ye assemble in some secret place and adore the spirit of Me, Queen of all Witcheries.

There shall ye assemble, who have not yet won my deepest secrets and are fain to learn all sorceries. To these shall I teach that which is yet unknown.

Ye shall be free from all slavery, and as a sign that you be free, ye shall be naked in your rites.

You shall sing, feast, make music and love, all in my presence, for mine is the ecstasy of the spirit, and mine is also joy upon earth.

My law is love unto all beings.

Mine is the secret that opens upon the door of youth, and mine is the cup of the wine of life, the cauldron of Cerridwen, which is the Holy Grail of Immortality.

I am the Gracious Goddess who gives the gift of youth unto the heart of mankind.

WITCHCRAFT

The number of practicing witches is increasing all the time. Wicca is steadily being accepted by society as a religion in its own right.

NOW AND IN

Wicca does, though, still face many challenges: From within, there are concerns about the direction the religion is taking; and, from the outside, there is still discrimination, ignorance, and prejudice against the whole notion of witchcraft. But, in just fifty years, Wicca has come a long way, and the future looks brighter still.

THE FUTURE

Modern Wicca

The new Wiccan religion has made huge strides in the United States and the rest of the world since it emerged in the 1950s. It has taken firm roots in a culture that already had a tradition of witchcraft, and is growing faster by the day—though just how fast it has grown is difficult to say.

Despite the surge of interest in witchcraft it is difficult to estimate the population of practitioners in the world. Most Wiccans are reluctant to publicize themselves, because there is discrimination against the craft in many societies, including in North America. Also, a substantial number of witches choose to work alone; they are known as "solitaries" or solitary witches. This means that even if we could ascertain the numbers of witches in organized covens, there would be many unaccounted for.

The structures of Wiccans outside individual covens are also deliberately loose, as many witches reject what they see as the hierarchical structures of monotheistic religions such as Christianity and Islam. Again, this means there are no centralized figures recorded of membership of "worship" as there may be in, say, the Catholic Church.

As a result of this uncertainty, estimates of the number of witches in different countries have varied enormously. For example, in the U.S. there have been estimates ranging from as few as just 4,000 witches, to an astonishing 5 million. Both these estimates can safely be regarded as wide of the mark. Taking into consideration the estimates of neopagan organizations, Christian organizations (who have their own reason for "exaggerating" the number of people practicing witchcraft), and other surveys, perhaps the safest estimate for the number of witches in the U.S. would be around 300,000 to 500,000. This figure should, however, be treated with caution, for the reasons already stated. Based on similar estimates, the population of witches in Canada may be around 30,000 to 50,000.

The picture in the rest of the world is equally unclear. For example, the 2011 UK census recorded approximately 85,000 people identifying as

∧ A Wiccan wedding, known as a "handfasting,"
takes place in Toronto in 2008, officiated by a priest
wearing ram's horns.

∧ The Ancient Order of Druids remains an influential
presence. Here, Druids gather to celebrate the summer
solstice at Stonehenge, with a midnight vigil, as well as
dawn and noon ceremonies.

pagan in the UK, with around 12,500 describing themselves as "Wicca." Other surveys, though, have come up with different figures. A similar picture emerges in other countries such as Australia and in Europe.

What Is Wicca?

One of the difficulties in knowing how many witches there are stems from defining who is, or is not, a witch. Surveys of witches sometimes include neopagans. Most, if not all, witches are neopagans, but not all neopagans are witches. Though Wicca has been described as the main strand of the neopagan movement that arose out of the 1950s and 1960s, there are a variety of others, including the Druid tradition.

Wiccans regard themselves as being part of a specific religion, albeit one with a variety of paths and traditions within it, as is the case with other religions such as Islam, Hinduism, and Christianity.

This view of Wicca as a legitimate religion has been gaining ground in society. In 1983 a U.S. district court ruled that a prisoner who wanted incense to carry out his Wiccan rituals was allowed to have it, and that by denying him the incense the Michigan Department of Corrections had violated the prisoner's right to freely exercise his religion under the First Amendment. In giving its ruling, the court implicitly accepted Wicca's status as a religion. Meanwhile, in 1985, the District Court of Virginia ruled that Wicca was a religion within the meaning of the First Amendment. This ruling was confirmed by judges from the Fourth Circuit Federal Appeals the following year.

The U.S. Army offically recognizes the Wicca religion and accords the estimated 10,000 or so army Wiccans the right to exercise their freedom of religious observance—though, as we shall see later, not without a great deal of controversy.

In Britain, where the modern witchcraft religion first emerged, there has been growing acceptance in some parts of society that Witchcraft is indeed a religion. For example, representatives from the Pagan Federation have recently sat on British government-organized bodies with other religious groups to discuss matters of faith in society. Early in 2002 a British college run by the Jesuit order of the Catholic Church hired a well-known British witch, the academic Dr. Vivianne Crowley, as a lecturer on the psychology of religion.

In both Britain and America there has been a huge growth in academic study, not just about the history of witchcraft, but on the contemporary phenomenon of Wicca too. But perhaps most striking of all has been the huge success of popular television programs over the past twenty years which feature witchcraft, such as *Sabrina the Teenage Witch*, *Buffy the Vampire Slayer*, its spin-off, *Angel*, and *Charmed*.

Though they vary enormously in their detail and bear little or no resemblance to real witchcraft, all these shows have one very important thing in common: They all portray witches (usually young, female, and attractive) in a positive light. While these shows and others like them may do little to explain the realities of witchcraft, they may then help dispel some of the traditional stereotyping of witches as "bad" people. Certainly, the number of young people seeking more information about witchcraft has markedly increased because of such shows, according to neopagan organizations.

What's in a Name?

One issue that Wicca has to face is the very question of which name to use to describe the craft and those who practice it. Many modern witches prefer to avoid the words "witch" and "witchcraft" altogether, for the simple reason that these words have held negative overtones for hundreds of years. Though attitudes are changing among some in society, still the mere mention of the word "witch" can alarm and alienate many people. It could be that Gerald Gardner, who developed

∧ A candlestick with pentagram marking, for use in a
neopagan, Wiccan or Druidic ritual.

∧ American neopagan and author Herman Slater (right)
performs a rite at his occult bookstore, the Magickal
Childe, in New York, 1981.

modern Wicca, may have seized upon the old word "Wicca" simply because it was not "Witchcraft"—and would therefore make the religion more palatable to a suspicious outside world.

Other witches take a different view. They are proud to be witches, and assert that the word "witch" should be reclaimed from those who taint it with misleading associations such as Satanism and devil worship. These witches feel that to abandon the word would be to forget the thousands who have died in history for being named as a witch.

This is one reason why some witches in both America and Britain do not describe themselves as Wiccan. Another reason is that they look toward other traditions, perhaps drawing on covens and practices that have developed independently of the Gardnerian tradition. There is also concern that some trends in modern-day Wicca are moving away from its essential nature as a initiatory, mystery religion.

In her book *The Heart of Wicca*, published in 2000, Ellen Cannon Reed, a Wiccan from California, comments on the fact that many Wiccans have lost sight of this traditional path of the religion.

She says, "There are lots of 'pagans' out there who don't even really believe in the Gods, lots of 'witches' who still practice Christianity, lots who call themselves 'pagan' or 'Wiccan' because they think it's cool, not because of any desire to follow a spiritual path."

Such views do sum up a significant minority of views among modern Wiccans. Basically, Wiccans have no problems with Christianity, except when it seeks to portray their faith in a misleading and sinister light, leading to discrimination. Most of the comments made by Wiccans are intended to illuminate the basic differences between the two belief systems. Christianity is monotheistic, priest-led, and strongly hierarchical, while Wicca is essentially polytheistic, individualistic, and flexible in its organization. Wicca also defines itself as featuring a personal process of initiation, plus expectations of continuing spiritual progress and increasing self-knowledge.

The media may have a central role here too. Although it was suggested earlier that programs such as *Sabrina the Teenage Witch* can help dispel some dangerous myths about witchcraft, some Wiccans see a risk that they will substitute other, perhaps equally insidious, myths. If, for example, these programs give young people the notion that witchcraft is simply about how to get a new boyfriend or how to get back at your enemy at school, then they will have done the true path of Wicca a disservice.

Opposition to Wicca

The dark days of the Burning Times have, of course, long gone in Western society. Yet the distant echoes of some of that—largely Christian— demonizing of witchcraft can still be heard in many parts of the world today. One of those places is the United States.

The courts may have upheld the rights of Wiccans to practice their religion freely, but the hearts and minds of many conservative Christian groups and politicians have not been won over so quickly. A good example of this was in 1999, when thirteen Christian groups in the U.S. proposed a Christian boycott of recruits to the U.S. Army, until the Army withdrew "all official support and approval from Witchcraft." The issue had arisen after publicity surrounding the religious practices of a coven of Wiccans at the Fort Hood military base in Texas.

The following words of Paul M. Weyrich, president of one of those conservative Christian groups, the Free Congress Association, were particularly significant. He said, "An Army that sponsors Satanic rituals is unworthy of representing the United States of America."

This familiar linkage of witchcraft and "Satanic rituals" indicates just how far Wiccans have yet to go to educate society about their true beliefs.

It is actually impossible for witches to be Satanists, since they do not believe in the Christian God–Devil duality. In a sense, only those who believe in Christianity can be Satanists.

∧   A contemporary image of witchcraft tools and symbols.

∧ Wicca continues to find converts to its message of
tolerance and respect for nature. Here, a modern witch
participates in Beltane rituals at Glastonbury
to celebrate the coming of summer.

The Future

These examples are important reminders that the Wicca religion is still under attack, fifty years after its recreation by Gerald Gardner, and a sign that its core beliefs have still not been grasped by large parts of society.

Yet on the whole the future looks a rosy one for modern pagan witchcraft. A number of organizations have sprung up that, though in no sense "running" Wicca, have nonetheless helped to coordinate the dissemination of information to potential initiates and the media. This in turn has helped counterbalance some of the more lurid accusations made against the craft.

With numbers of witches increasing, it is also no surprise that sales of literature concerning witchcraft have also continued to rise, even if some of the material on sale is far removed from the traditions of true witchcraft. Wicca is not an evangelical religion, and most Wiccans accept that their way is one of the many paths that humans can tread on the way to spiritual health. Tolerance and respect for others, as well as a deep reverence for nature and the earth they live on, are fundamental to modern witches.

Wiccans are not looking to establish one world religion. All they ask is that they be allowed to practice their beliefs as they choose without facing discrimination, and without having those beliefs misleadingly represented. After the long, broken, and often bloody history of witchcraft, that is a modest but important hope, and one that increasingly looks as if it will be granted.

CONCLUSION

The Ethics of Wicca

Witchcraft differs from other religions in that it does not have a detailed set of rules of conduct for followers. Part of the essence of Wicca is, in fact, that it does not believe that humans should be burdened by guilt from concepts such as original sin, but, rather, that people should instead enjoy the full pleasures that life and nature have to offer. This does not mean, however, that Wiccans are encouraged to do whatever they please, whatever the consequences. Wicca does have one central tenet. Known as the "Wiccan Rede" or "Witches' Rede," it is as follows:

An it harm none, do what you will.

In this context "an" simply means "as long as" or simply "if." The Rede is sometimes stated in more archaic language using the words "thy will." It is a deceptively simple rule, and one much debated by Wiccans. Some find it restrictive, pointing out that it is next to impossible to go through life without harming others, including yourself. Some Wiccans have countered this by saying that one meaning of the word "Rede" is "advice." In this sense the Rede is a guideline, not a rigid law. Other Wiccans find the Rede liberating, a welcome change in their view from the gloomy and guilt-ridden moralizing of some other religions, and believe that witches should feel happy about enjoying the pleasures that life has to offer without feeling ashamed.

Yet another point of view is that the Rede stresses a key element at the heart of witchcraft: self-responsibility. Though Wiccans generally prefer to practice in groups and the coven for many is essential to witchcraft, ultimately all witches have to accept responsibility for their behavior, and have to seek their own personal path to spiritual growth and development and union with nature. At the heart of Wicca is each individual's own relationship with the divine. Witches are encouraged to develop their own powers, creativity, and personality, but not at the expense of other people.

WHAT WITCHES BELIEVE

The beliefs of modern witches can vary considerably or from individual to individual. Many people are attracted to Witchcraft because they like its lack of dogma and its emphasis on personal development. However, there are some core beliefs at the heart of modern Witchcraft that most witches adhere to.

———— ✳ ————

The Goddess and the God

Witches believe in a deity, which is ultimately neither male nor female. The deity manifests itself in female and male polarity—the Goddess and the God. The Goddess, in particular, is at the heart of witchcraft religion. The Goddess, or Lady, represents nature, Mother Earth, fertility, the endless cycle of life. Her consort, the God—often represented as the Horned God—shares this role of symbolizing life, death, and rebirth. Some witches choose to place less emphasis on the male aspect of the deity.

The Goddess and God are also revered in the forms of gods and goddesses from the old pagan religions. This might be, for example, Isis, Diana, or the Celtic goddess Danu. These represent facets of the Goddess and God, and are both personalities in their own right and archetypes of age-old natural forces.

Witches believe that the divine is both within and outside us, and that we are all ultimately children of the Goddess. They also believe in reincarnation.

Nature

A reverence for nature is also central to modern Witchcraft. Witches aim to respect the laws of nature, and to live in harmony with the world around them.

The Central Myth of Witchcraft

The core myth in modern Witchcraft is the endless cycle of life—sometimes called the Myth of Rebirth or just the Myth of the Goddess. One ancient version of this story is that of Persephone, who travels down to the Underworld for part of the year (winter) only to return later to the surface of the earth (spring/summer).

An essential point about this story of life, death, and rebirth is that the death/darkness is equally as important as the other aspects. Witches do not fear this darkness but embrace it as part of the whole cycle. The cycle is symbolized also by the moon—the waxing, waning, and full moons. This is sometimes represented by the triple aspects of the Goddess—the Maiden (waxing moon), Mother (full), and Crone (waning).

Role of Ritual and Magic

Personal development is a key part of modern Witchcraft, and this is achieved in part by being in communion with the gods. This is the role of witches' rituals—to help individuals raise their consciousness to commune with the divine.

For many witches the casting of spells is an important part of their identity as a witch. Some, however, concentrate almost exclusively on the spiritual and personal development aspects of modern Witchcraft.

∧ An engraving by Agostino Veneziano (c.1490–1540) shows a female witch riding on an animal skeleton, preceded by two men and a boy on a goat blowing on a horn.

GLOSSARY

Amulet: object that is given magical powers and protects the wearer from bad luck and evil spirits.

Artemis: Greek goddess worshipped throughout the ancient world; the goddess of nature.

Astarte or Ashtoreth: Phoenician goddess of fertility and war.

Athame: black-handled knife used in magic for focusing a person's will and drawing shapes such as magic circles and pentagrams.

Beltane: festival on April 30 or May 1, one of the four major festivals of the year for witches.

Book of Shadows: the book of rituals and spells followed by a coven or individual witch.

Burning Times: name given to the period of the late Middle Ages and early modern period when thousands of alleged witches were executed—often by being burned alive.

Cauldron: vessel used by modern witches in magic rituals, symbolizing change and transformation.

Cernunnos: the Celtic Horned God depicted as a man with a bull's or stag's horns.

Chanting: in magic rituals the chanting of sacred names or words is used to help raise consciousness and psychic power.

Charms: words or phrases used in magical spells, often written on paper or other objects.

Coven: a group of witches who meet together on a regular basis; traditionally the number in a coven is thirteen.

Cunning folk: the name used in Britain and North America from the sixteenth century for people who practice simple or folk magic.

Cybele: Mother Earth goddess, the Roman equivalent of the Greek goddess Rhea.

Demons: name used for spirits that are intermediaries between the material world and the world of the gods; in Christian tradition they became associated purely with evil and specifically the Devil.

Devil: in Christianity the repository of pure evil and set up by Christians as the counterbalance to Jesus Christ.

Diana: Roman goddess of hunting and wild things, and revered by many witches as representing the fiercely independent Goddess beholden to no man.

Dionysus: Greek god of wine and nature whose followers took part in secret and lavish initiation ceremonies, the Dionysian Rites.

Dunking: term used for telling whether people were witches by immersing them in water; if they floated they were witches.

Esbat: name for regular meetings of a coven of witches, usually but not always held at the full moon.

Fairies: supernatural spirits who inhabit the realms between earth and Heaven and may be either good or bad.

Gardnerian: tradition of modern Witchcraft developed by the British civil servant Gerald Gardner in the 1950s.

Green Man: in European mythology a deity or spirit of nature, especially vegetation; other names include Green George and Jack-in-the-Green.

Grimoire: book containing magical spells passed down through generations from as far back as the Middle Ages.

Hecate: powerful Greek goddess associated with magic and the Underworld and who is often depicted as a Triple Goddess.

Hex: name for a spell, coming from Pennsylvania Dutch and based on an old German word for witch.

High priestess: in modern Witchcraft the leader of a coven, assisted by the high priest.

Horned God: old Celtic god, revered in modern Witchcraft as male consort to the Goddess.

Imbolc: festival on February 2, one of four major festivals for witches.

Ishtar: much-worshipped Mother Goddess of the Assyrian and Babylonian cultures linked with the Underworld and the cycle of life, death, and rebirth.

Isis: Egyptian goddess who tricked Ra into giving her immortality; sister and wife of Osiris and mother of Horus.

Kabbalah (also spelt Kabala, Qabalah): the Jewish system of philosophy and mystical writings widely read by magicians in the nineteenth century.

Knot: the use of tying and untying knots to bind and release magical energy is widespread in witchcraft.

Lilith: by tradition, the first wife of Adam, who went off in anger when she was denied equal rights; she became a demon preying on newborn children.

Lughnasadh: one of four major annual festivals for witches, observed on July 31, named after the Celtic god Lugh. Also known as Lammas.

Magic circle: sacred area created by witches in which magic rituals and ceremonies take place.

***Malleus Maleficarum*:** fifteenth-century manual that set out how witches should be tried and punished.

Maleficia: Latin term meaning harmful or bad acts of magic.

Medea: Greek witch with great magical powers who helped Jason and the Argonauts retrieve the Golden Fleece;

her bad reputation came after she killed their two children in revenge when Jason went off with another woman.

Pan: Greek god of nature, often depicted as half man and half goat, now revered by witches as an aspect of the Horned God.

Pricking: method adopted in the late Middle Ages for testing whether someone was a witch; it was assumed that witches had a special mark that was insensitive to pain.

Sabbats: in history, the nocturnal meetings at which the Devil and witches met; now the name used by many modern witches for their seasonal festivals.

Samhain: one of the most important of the four major Celtic festivals, held on October 31.

Satan: common alternative name for the Devil, which has led to the word "Satanism."

Satanism: the worship of the Devil, wrongly ascribed to witches in the late Middle Ages and at other periods.

Scrying: the craft or art of clairvoyance, often carried out with a crystal ball or other objects with a smooth, shiny surface in which the future can be foreseen.

Selene: Greek goddess of the moon; in modern witchcraft she is often seen as one aspect of the Triple Goddess, the others being Hecate and Artemis.

Shamanism: system of magic and healing in which the shaman enters an altered state of consciousness to commune with spirits, to help achieve his goal.

Sky-clad: usual name for the nudity preferred by many witches during rituals.

Solitary: a witch who practices alone rather than as part of a coven.

Spell: formula of words either written or spoken, intended to cause an action.

Talisman: object that possesses magic powers in its own right, which can be transferred or transmitted to its owner.

Warlock: popular term for a male witch, though shunned by most practitioners; it comes from an Anglo-Saxon origin meaning "oath-breaker."

Wicca: name given to the modern Witchcraft religion by its founder or re-creator Gerald Gardner.

Wiccan Rede: the simple rule by which modern witches live, that they can do what they like as long as it doesn't hurt anyone.

Witch craze: name given to the widespread persecution of alleged witches in the late Middle Ages and early modern period in Europe and North America.

Wizard: old word, rarely used now, for a folk witch and also applied to male magicians.

INDEX

INDEX

Brimming with creative inspiration, how-to projects and useful information to enrich your everyday life, Quarto Knows is a favourite destination for those pursuing their interests and passions. Visit our site and dig deeper with our books into your area of interest: Quarto Creates, Quarto Cooks, Quarto Homes, Quarto Lives, Quarto Drives, Quarto Explores, Quarto Gifts, or Quarto Kids.

First published in 2020 by White Lion Publishing, an imprint of The Quarto Group.
The Old Brewery, 6 Blundell Street
London, N7 9BH,
United Kingdom
T (0)20 7700 6700 F (0)20 7700 8066
www.QuartoKnows.com

Text © 2020 Quarto

Every effort has been made to trace the copyright holders of material quoted in this book. If application is made in writing to the publisher, any omissions will be included in future editions.

A catalogue record for this book is available from the British Library.

ISBN 978-0-7112-5224-0
10 9 8 7 6 5 4 3 2 1

Typeset in Sabon and Regulator Nova
Design by Isabel Eeles

Printed in China

page 15: *Saul and the Witch of Endor* (1870) by Gustave Doré; **page 35:** *Circe the Sorceress turns Odysseus' Men into Swine and Sends them to the Styes* (1907) by Henry Justice Ford; **page 53:** *The Massacre of the Druids* (*c.*1850) by John Rogers; **page 67:** *Witch Riding Backwards on a Goat Accompanied by Four Putti* (*c.*1505) by Albrecht Dürer; page 86: "The Wheel of the Year"; **page 91:** *The Fall of the Rebel Angels* (1866) by Gustave Doré; **page 107:** *The Burning of Witches in Medieval Times* (1883); **page 137:** *Hexenritt* (1870) by Gustav Adolph Spangenberg; **page 149:** *The Trial of Two Witches in Salem* (1892) by Howard Pyle; **page 170:** *The Blazing Pentagram* (1854) by Éliphas Lévi; **page 175:** *The Great Symbol of Salomon* (1860); **page 191:** *Rosicrucian Compass* (1779) by Eugen Lennhoff; **page 210:** *A Witches' Sabbat* (*c.*1650); **page 213:** *Eleanor Doing Penance for Witchcraft* (1789) by Anker Smith; **page 229:** *A Witch Placing a Scorpion into a Pot in Order to Make a Potion* (n.d.) by F. Landerer, after M. Schmidt

Picture credits